A GUIDE TO THE STONE CIRCLES OF CUMBRIA

Robert W. E. Farrah

O send out thy light and thy truth: let them lead me;
let them bring me unto thy holy hill, and to thy *'stone circles'*.
Psalm xliii, 3.

HAYLOFT

THE STONE CIRCLES OF CUMBRIA

And if thou wilt make me an altar of stone, thou shalt not build it of hewn stone: for if thou lift up thy tool upon it, thou hast polluted it. Exodus xx, 25

I will sit also upon the mount of the congregation, in the sides of the north: I will ascend above the heights of the clouds; I will be like the most High. Isaiah xiv, 13-14

You have noticed that everything an Indian does is in a circle, and that is because the Power of the World always works in circles, and everything tries to be round. In the old days when we were a strong and happy people, all our power came to us from the sacred hoop of the nation, and so long as the hoop was unbroken, the people flourished. The flowering tree was the living centre of the hoop, and the circle of the four quarters nourished it. The east gave peace and light, the south gave warmth, the west gave rain, and the north with its cold and mighty wind, gave strength and endurance. This knowledge came to us from the outer world with our religion. Everything the Power of the World does is done in a circle. The sky is round, and I have heard that the earth is round like a ball, and so are all the stars. The wind, in its greatest power, whirls. Birds make their nests in circles, for theirs is the same religion as ours. The sun comes forth and goes down again in a circle. The moon does the same, and both are round. Even the seasons form a great circle in their changing, and always come back again to where they were. The life of a man is a circle from childhood to childhood, and so it is in everything where power moves. Our teepees were round like the nests of birds, and these were always set in a circle, the nation's hoop, a nest of many nests, where the Great Spirit meant for us to hatch our children.

Nicholas Black Elk (Hehaka Sapa), *The Great Circle* (Mandala)

The Bard, Thomas Jones, 1774.
By kind permission of the
National Museum of Wales

First published 2008

Hayloft Publishing Ltd, Kirkby Stephen,
Cumbria, CA17 4DJ

tel: + 44 (0) 17683) 42300
fax. + 44 (0) 17683) 41568
e-mail: books@hayloft.eu
web: www.hayloft.eu

ISBN 1 904524 53 2

A catalogue record for this book is available
from the British Library

Printed and bound in the EU

Papers used by Hayloft are natural, recyclable products made from wood grown in sustainable forests.
The manufacturing processes conform to the environmental regulations of the country of origin.

Contents

ILLUSTRATIONS

In the Guide:
All photographs and plans within the guide are by the author except the Map: Locations of Stone Circles and the embanked plans of Banniside, The Beacon, Casterton, The Kirk and The Cockpit by Scruffy Crow 2006.

An additional source of photographs of many of the stone circles listed in this guide can be accessed on www.google.co.uk using the Google Image Search.

ACKNOWLEDGEMENTS

THE IDEA FOR this guide originated at the exhibition 'Stone Circles and Standing Stones of Eden' at Penrith Museum in 2002. The demand for further information on the stone circles by visitors to the exhibition resulted in the present work. My thanks to Judith Clarke and Syd Chaplin, the curators of the museum, for their encouragement and criticism during the early stages.

I was indebted to many during the research and writing of this guide – early and modern antiquarians, archaeologists and independent researchers; all works which are relevant to the guide have been listed in the bibliography.

In particular this book has benefited from the expert attention of numerous individuals. My research has been informed by the archaeologist Dr. Aaron Watson, who kindly allowed me to read the unpublished manuscript *On the edge of England: Cumbria as a Neolithic region* and also for the recommendation of some primary sources.

Thanks also to the Curators of the Royal Commission on the Ancient and Historical Monuments of Scotland (RCAHMS) for their response to my enquiries concerning the Thom Archives and especially to Dr Ian Fraser at RCAHMS for his help on the Thom Archive and for his compiling of a basic listing of the Thom Notebooks and thanks to Eoghann MacColl for permission to allow access to the Thom Archive. Thanks are due to Dr James Deboo for his help with the manuscript.

To my dear friend and megalithic artist Brian Cowper and his wife Joanne for providing inspiration, encouragement and companionship. To our many sojourns amongst the stones and those silences…

And lastly to my wife Carole... if the moon had a sister...

Robert Farrah, September 2007

PREFACE

I BOARD A high speed train at Lancaster and take a seat. Since Robert Farrah first asked me to write a foreword for this guide I have regularly travelled by rail through the hills to Penrith. I reflect on this as the train gathers speed past Morecambe Bay, looking out across the sands to the Lake District fells. These mountains were of great significance to the people who walked this land over four thousand years ago. Not only were they the setting for some of the largest Neolithic stone quarries in Britain, but also the focus for one of the greatest concentrations of stone circles. Even now, far to the west, the distinctive profile of Black Combe points the way to the stones of Swinside.

Beyond Oxenholme the train enters the spectacular Lune Gorge, a significant routeway in both the past and the present. For me the Lune Gorge marks a major transition in the journey as the lowlands are replaced by a more rugged upland landscape. As the valley opens towards Orton my eyes seek out the location of Gamelands, where a stone circle of pink granite contrasts against white limestone outcrops. The train now climbs towards Shap, skirting the low hills that surround the Oddendale and Iron Hill circles. I catch a glimpse of the ruins of Kemp Howe, a stone circle destroyed when the railway was cut through its centre. Among nearby houses and fields lie fragments of a once impressive stone avenue, while a saddle on the skyline marks Moor Divock, a cluster of Bronze Age cairns and circles.

Just out of sight of the concentric rings of Gunnerkeld the train begins its long descent towards Penrith. A tremendous vista opens across the Vale of Eden and I can make out the distant hills where one of Britain's largest stone circles, Long Meg and Her Daughters, is located. On the final approach to Penrith the boulder-built banks of Mayburgh henge rise across the fields, framed by Cross Fell. Even from this distance, Mayburgh's setting under the wide skies of Eden is impressive. In the opposite direction a distinct break in the mountainous skyline between Helvellyn and Blencathra shows the way to Castlerigg, perhaps the most dramatic circle of them all.

Stepping down onto the platform at Penrith I consider how my journey has been orchestrated by the land and the prehistoric places set within it. While the view from a train might seem far removed from the lives of the circle-builders of prehistory, it emphasises to me how their legacy is now a part of the modern world. In this, the first comprehensive gazetteer of Cumbrian stone circles to be published for many years, Robert Farrah also reveals that these enigmatic places are not only the province of archaeology or the imagination. Stone circles are out there in the landscape to be visited and experienced first hand, and this guide is an invaluable resource for anyone wishing to make their own journeys to these remarkable monuments.

Aaron Watson, 2006

Introduction

SOME 12,000 YEARS ago, the modern county of Cumbria, which contains the Lake District National Park, lay dormant beneath a vast sheet of ice with only the peaks of the highest fells still visible. These were the last glaciations of an ice age which was beginning to recede due to the advance of a more temperate climate, which brought a gradual greening of the land. Amongst post-glacial moraines and tundra, lichens and mosses began slowly to colonise and alchemise the soil. As the surface of the earth grew richer, the land deepened in colour and scents. Small trees and bushes began to appear on the grasslands; birch and pine, followed by oak, hazel, lime and elm. A tangle of scrub and woodland developed. Vast tracts of forest spread along the fertile valleys, over moorland and fell and then up steeper inclines of the mountains, reaching heights of 750m (2,500ft) in places.

Some time prior to the ninth millennium BC, the first people landed along the estuaries and coasts. These were the hunters and gatherers of the Mesolithic, a nomadic people who exploited the seasonal resources of sea and land. The Mesolithic people settled along the coastal margins between the sea and forest, and on the limestone uplands in the south. Their presence is determined by scatters of flint and stone, sometimes found alongside the remains of shells and the bones of both wild and domestic herds. These nomadic people exploited seasonal resources of food, living off the fat of the land, following the migrating herds and the naturally-occurring flora and fauna. They laid down the first routes through the landscape in their seasonal pursuit, following natural contours along the sides of valleys, rivers and their terraces into the hinterlands and back to the sea. Then, some 6,000 years ago, people began to settle the land. This was the beginning of the Neolithic – the New Stone Age. Many locations have shown a continuity of activity from the Mesolithic to the Neolithic. This continuity, the later Neolithic following in the footsteps of the earlier Mesolithic, showed that there was some cohesion between the two periods. The Neolithic is categorised by a new stone technology which resulted in a better-developed and more powerful axe. Inroads were made into the scrub and forest, woodland was cleared for settlement, land for grazing and fields for crops. Neolithic people became the first to farm the land, resulting in some control over the environment and in turn a new-found freedom which would lead to better cultural developments. It was late in the Neolithic period that the first stone circles began to appear.

Cumbria is the most mountainous region of England. The lakes for which the Lake District is named, are to be found in the glaciated valleys which spread out like the spokes of a wheel from the central dome. The mountains of this central massif, within the bounds of the National Park, occupy an area of 2243 square kilometres (866 square miles), consisting of Borrowdale Volcanics which are bordered to the north by the Skiddaw slates and to the south by the Silurian shales. The central massif is surrounded by an almost continuous ring of lower Carboniferous limestone fells, broken only in the south by the estuaries of the Leven and Kent where the older Silurian shales are found exposed. To the north the Carboniferous limestone hills lower to the Carlisle plain which consists of Triassic rocks covered by glacial deposits.

NOTE: See glossary at the end of the guide for explanations of any unfamiliar terms.

To the east the hills lower to the River Eden. Between the Eden and the Pennines is a band of Traissic sandstone which gradually broadens as it moves northwards towards the Carlisle plain. The mountainous central area is surrounded by a ring of fertile lowlands which became the main areas of settlement. To the north, west and south this fertile tract of land is between seven to twenty kilometres (4.3 to 12.4 miles) wide which gradually lowers to the coastal plain. To the east is the valley of the river Eden, up to twelve kilometres (7.4 miles) at its widest, separating the Cumbrian mountains from the Pennines. With few exceptions, mainly glacial erratics, the stone used in the construction of circles usually mirrors the local geology.

The advent of Romanticism first attracted visitors to the lakes as pilgrims of a new enlightenment. The movement was inspired by painters, poets and philosophers, who made this landscape of lakes, fearful mountains, mists and vapours their spiritual home. They came in search of the sublime and the picturesque, with a passion for wild landscapes of 'beauty, horror and immensity', all bathed in an 'out-of-this-world sunset glow – a land touched by heaven'. This transcendent vision of the landscape may have influenced our own perceptions but such reverence for the land is evident in many ancient societies. Mountainous regions in particular were regarded as holy ground and their sacred heights the kingdoms of gods. They were a 'residence for the supernatural' (MacFarlane, 2003) and the genesis of spiritual revelation which became the foundation of many faiths worldwide. So the Romantic vision can be seen to be intuitive rather than an innovation, complying with a more archaic sensibility. The stone circles widely held to be of druidic origin at this time were an integral feature of this visionary landscape, although there is no real evidence to connect the stone circles to the druids.

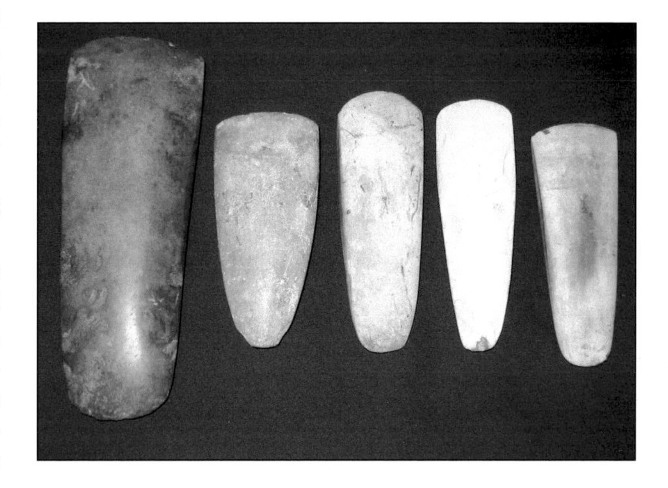

The origins of this assumption are to be found in Julius Caesar's account of the Gallic War, *De Bello Gallico,* where he writes concerning the druidic order that, 'Besides this, they have many discussions as touching the stars and their movement, the size of the universe and of the earth, the order of nature, the strength and powers of the immortal gods'. The later Romantic interest in the druidic can be traced back to the antiquarian John Aubrey in the seventeenth century, and a link between druids and stone circles 'became almost universally accepted' following the publications of *Stonehenge* and *Abury* by William Stukeley in the eighteenth century (Michell, 1982). The theories of these early antiquarians attributed such astronomical, mathematical and mystical properties as Caesar had described the druids as possessing to the stone circles, and so the monuments were perceived to be the temples of the druids. The ascendancy of druidism and its connection with the stone circles was very much a part of the Romantic vision. Their proximity to the central dome of mountains was a setting revered by the Romantics who intuitively connected them to an ancient vision of transcendence.

Left, Swinside Stone Circle from the north west. This page, Neolithic stone axes at Tullie House Museum, Carlisle.

The stones of the 'Druid Temple' Castlerigg and other monuments were often painted white in order to 'give the stones a moonlit, ghastly, sublime effect' (Lefebure, 1987). It is likely that the trees on the banks of Mayburgh Henge were planted at this time to comply with this vision of the sublime and picturesque. The Romantic vision was also very likely responsible for influencing Colonel Lacy in his restoration of Long Meg and her Daughters so that 'a proper view of the whole circle could be had' (Burl, 1999). Without this restoration it is likely that the circle would not have made such an intense impression upon Wordsworth, who stated that, 'I have not seen any other relique of those dark ages which can pretend to rival it in singularity and dignity of appearance'. The Romantic vision saw these ancient sites as the embodiment of atmospheres at once magical, other-worldly and elemental, retaining a power to fascinate. Wordsworth writes that,

A weight of awe not easy to be borne
Fell suddenly upon my spirit,

when unexpectedly he had come upon Long Meg and her Daughters, and as the morning, 'dispels the cumbrous shades of Night'

That wondrous Monument, whose mystic round
Forth shadows, some have deemed, to mortal sight
The inviolable God that tames the proud.

Despite the encroachment of modern industry, suburbia and the increase of traffic, these ancient sites still retain this numinous atmosphere which was so important to the early visitors who came in search of these wild subliminal places. The purpose of this guide is to allow the visitor to discover these 'Druid Temples' and the visionary landscapes that inspired such deep veneration.

The stone circles of Cumbria have incomparable locations – some of the finest are a dominant feature of the historic landscape. It has been estimated that Cumbria possesses 65 surviving stone circles – a fifth of all the circles to be found in England, making it a region of significant megalithic importance. Many have disappeared; systematically broken up, a quarry for buildings, roads and the walls of enclosures, their presence also proved an inconvenience for the plough (see Appendix I). Such activity undoubtedly provided the cloak at times for a more fundamental intolerance, the spiritual fanaticism of zealots. A visit to that once 'stupendous monument of antiquity' Kemp Howe and the Shap Avenue or the Gretigate stone circles will deepen our regret for all the other circles which have disappeared from the landscape.

The region's relative geographical isolation, with the Irish Sea to the west, the Solway Firth to the north, the Pennines to the east and Morecambe Bay to the south, has been cited as a reason for this strong megalithic presence. But this island mentality belongs to a wider geographic area. Cumbria is one of many important Neolithic regions around the Irish Sea, including 'north Wales, south-west Scotand, the Isle of Man and eastern Ireland' (Watson & Bradley, in press). Indeed, Neolithic stone axes which were quarried within the Cumbrian fells have been found throughout all these regions. But there are other characteristics which suggest common regional traditions: the design traits of the early circles like Castlerigg, Long Meg, Gunnerkeld, Brat's Hill and Swineside find a similarity with Ballynoe, Co. Down, almost

The Druidical Circle, near Keswick, J. B. Pyne, 1859.

The Druids' Stones, near Keswick, Thomas Allom.

directly west from Swineside across the Irish Sea (Burl, 2000); the large embanked enclosure of Mayburgh Henge in the Eden Valley does not conform to any other known type of henge on mainland Britain but does bear some resemblance to the later Neolithic enclosures of the Boyne Valley in County Meath; these Irish sites also seem to possess a similar preference for elevated locations.

Lastly, the very localised rock art found in the Eden Valley and nearby is quite unique, differing from neighbouring regions where such art is found mainly on horizontal outcrops of rock. Many stones are highly decorated with motifs such as cup and ring, concentric rings, spirals and chevrons and are 'highly unusual in northern Britain'(Beckensall, 2002; Watson & Bradley, in press), but they can be found decorating the kerbstones of the passage graves like Knowth and Newgrange in the Boyne Valley.

The circles of Cumbria were constructed over a period of two millennia, from the late Neolithic to the middle of the Bronze Age. Generally, the earliest circles were built on the lower valley plains in and around the central dome of mountains and the later ones occupy more elevated hillside positions. In the south and west the circles are found along the coastal plain and the lower hills, whereas those in the north and east are found along the Eden Valley.

Journeying between the communities around the coastal plain of the south and west would have been a fairly simple undertaking. To the north and east the River Eden provided an important prehistoric route which gave access to the broad, fertile valley of the Eden.

The central Lakeland and Howgill fells effectively isolated the two regions, which resulted in some vernacular characteristics. This is particularly true of the smaller and later circles, reflecting a more personalised usage by smaller communities. Building these monuments with manpower alone must have required considerable effort, time and organisation. That they have endured in the landscape is a potent reminder of their importance. Such investments of labour testify to the value the communities placed on them, often suggesting more perennial, possibly ritualistic motives, far beyond the practicalities of necessity.

Stone circles are a mysterious synthesis of place and feeling where the past and present, the known and unknown, the seen and unseen all have a presence. By their very nature they will always challenge our understanding of their full purposes. Their mystery is part of their attraction; however, some explanations have been persuasively given. Of one thing we can be certain: a circle's situation was the product of planning and consultation – it was purposefully located. This is why our understanding of the monument's environment is so important, because some of a stone circle's mystery is encoded in the land and sky.

A possible unifying factor in the distribution of the stone circles and henges are the localities of a Neolithic industry within the central Cumbrian fells – the 'stone axe factory' sites. The main sources of the correct stone within the Cumbrian massif are all accessible by valley routes from the lowlands and it is in those areas 'that we find the earliest archaeological and environmental evidence of settlement and land use' (Bradley & Edmonds, 2005). The Langdales were the most significant of these areas, the largest producer of Neolithic stone axes in Britain. Many roughed-out stone axes were found in the Langdale 'factories', the first of which were discovered in 1947, but since then numerous sites have been identified in the central fells.

The exploitation of these sites occur from around 4000 to 2200 BC. The earliest stone circles appeared in this period, and the archaeologist W. G. Collingwood suggested that 'the stone circles and the axes thus hang together'. The trade in axes appears to have been conducted over large distances, for they have been found in many places in the British Isles.

The location of large stone circles has been persuasively linked with the distribution of the stone axes (Burl, 2000). The distribution of many monuments may be connected with the routes used to trade the axes, many being found to command access routes into the mountains. The regularity with which the stone circles are located around the perimeter of the central fells suggests that the rings possibly served as staging posts in the trade of axes. The distance between the circles and the distance between the circles and the factory sites suggests an attempt at a uniform arrangement (Burl, 2000).

Cup and ring markings on a stone at Penrith Museum, Peter Koronka.

The stone axe was a valued tool and it's likely that source and supply were regulated. Many of the factory sites are to be found in very exposed mountain locations, places of danger and uncertainty, and these may have been purposefully chosen to protect them and make them difficult to access. It is possible that their whereabouts, veiled in secrecy, were known only to those who controlled and allowed entry. The very inaccessibility and isolation of the sources of stone, the journey and the labour needed to acquire it, have also been interpreted in a spiritual context, as if some aesthetic value was placed upon it. Why quarry for the stone towards the summit of a mountain when 'equally suitable rock was available in far more accessible and hospitable locations?' (Bradley & Edmonds, 2005). Axes were promethean, instruments of transformation both as hardware and symbol. They were multi-functional: a means of clearing the land of its tangle of wood and scrub to allow settlement and farming; they provided the wood for the fires at the heart of the homestead; they were also very effective weapons that could easily take a life.

But there is also evidence which suggests that they were regarded in a more symbolic context. Some axes are too small, delicate or large to have been of any practical use. Others have been highly polished, suggesting more aesthetic

Shap Avenue, in the 18th century, painting by Lady Lowther

concerns with the grain and colour of the stone. Many have been found in such large numbers in rivers, bogs and springs that they seem to have been purposefully placed or thrown there as votive offerings. Axes are also found carved on many megalithic monuments. Stone circles are often located on lower fells between the high isolated mountains of the interior and the coastal plains, possibly marking the beginning of a perilous journey to acquire precious stone. In 1988 a count was made of Langdale stone axes; 1,512 have been found and recorded throughout Britain, an impressive 39% of all stone axes found, testimony to the importance of the trade and possibly an indication of the prestige in which the area was held in megalithic times.

The first stone circles appeared by the beginning of the late Neolithic, around 3200BC, and continued into the early Bronze Age, around 1600BC. The stone circle has an enduring tradition spanning some two millennia. Because of this long tradition, it was inevitable that some diversity in size, design and shape occurred. However, the interpretation of this variety of features to establish a chronological sequence of evolution has proven to be problematic. The most useful remains for the dating of stone circles are those obtained from organic remains or artefacts. But very few have had dates determined using organic material because many circles were excavated prior to reliable dating techniques being available. Pottery found in association with burials has proved more useful. Precise categorisation needs to be treated with some caution; rigid classifications of sites have been criticised because they often disguise a series of phases during the evolution of a monument. The chronological evidence is sometimes somewhat ambiguous. It is likely that, in some instances, for example, some circles have had a longer sequence of usage than any associated finds. The classification of monuments is mostly reliant upon the visible remains and it is important to recognise that, 'Without adequate excavation... the present form of the monument may only represent a final phase, and there may have been complex sequences of development...' (Clare, 2007). A later monument may incorporate an earlier one. 'A critical issue is that we should be careful not to impose specific ways of viewing monuments that are solely determined by abstract representations' (Watson, 2004b).

However, some circles do appear to follow rules of classification enabling a general categorisation. It is commonly accepted that the larger stone circles precede the smaller, later circles, and that circles with large stones, entrances with portal stones and outliers are properties which are likely to belong to the earlier circles. These early circles, such as Castlerigg, Long Meg, Swineside and the now destroyed Grey Yauds are thought possibly to predate or to be contemporary with the earliest phases of Stonehenge. Circles of smaller stones and those associated with burials are thought to be later. Burl has attempted to construct a 'diagnostic scheme' based upon the features of stone circles, which seems to give 'a crude but apparently reliable indication of the chronological relationship of the circle' (Burl, 2000).

Several types of stone circle have been identified by an analysis of these traits and are given in the order they are thought to have evolved. The earliest of these are the great open circles, the classic stone circle consisting of standing stones surrounding a large open inner area; these often have an entrance defined by portal stones. The embanked stone circle is a circle of standing stones surrounded by an earthen bank. The concentric stone circle consists of one or more circles which share a common centre. Cairn circles consisting of a kerb of larger standing stones at the base of and near the perimeter of a cairn, which helped to contain the smaller stones covering the burial. Lastly another embanked circle is a circular bank of earth with stones showing above the bank and sometimes on the inner and outer edges of the bank; these surround a small inner area (see Fig 1, page 20). The embanked circle is structurally

Mickleden and Oxendale from the top of Pike O'Stickle scree, Gabriel Blamires

closely associated with the embanked stone circle. Some caution needs to be exercised because the archaeological record has demonstrated that some circles have been shown to predate accompanying burials, the latter showing evidence of continuity and interest in an older monument, while some cairn circles have been shown to be contemporary with the earlier circles. Burl's 'diagnostic scheme' shows that categorisation can be a useful descriptive tool but, as Clare and Watson have quite correctly observed, some discretion is needed in imposing our own values and criteria upon the past. Clare has recently suggested that '... it is worth restating the possibility that the differences between stone circles... may be functional and hierarchical rather than just chronological.' (Clare, 2007).

Not all stone circles are truly circular. The pioneering surveys of a retired Professor of Engineering, Alexander Thom, were to further an awareness of the architectural properties of stone circles, and these surveys are his most enduring legacy. In these surveys the stones are usually highlighted against the background of a fine spider's web of pencilled geometries showing Thom's proposed methods of construction. In his notebooks each individual stone of a circle is drawn and its statistics carefully mapped and measured. There are some twenty pages for Swinside, 27 for Castlerigg and 29 for Long Meg. There are 99 notebooks held in the archives of the Royal Commission on the Ancient and Historical Monuments of Scotland commencing in 1939 and running almost consecutively until 1978 (see Appendix II).

Thom surveyed 26 of the stone circles in this guide (see Appendix III). Thom's studies highlighted various geometric shapes of 'circle'. Four main categories of circle were identified: the true circle which predominates, the flattened circle, the ellipse and the egg. The true circle outnumbers its nearest rivals, the flattened circles, by approximately four to one. Thom recognized two main types of flattened circle, identifying them as Type A and Type B, both differing in their geometric construction. He further identified a flattened circle which was a slight modification which he called a Type D. There was a Type C but it differed only slightly in its construction to a Type B. Thom became convinced that it was a variant of the latter and so Type C became a modified Type B. He also determined three types of egg as Type I, Type II and Type III (Thom,1967; Thom & Thom, 1978; Heggie, 1981). These designs are also thought to comply approximately with the chronological sequence in which they

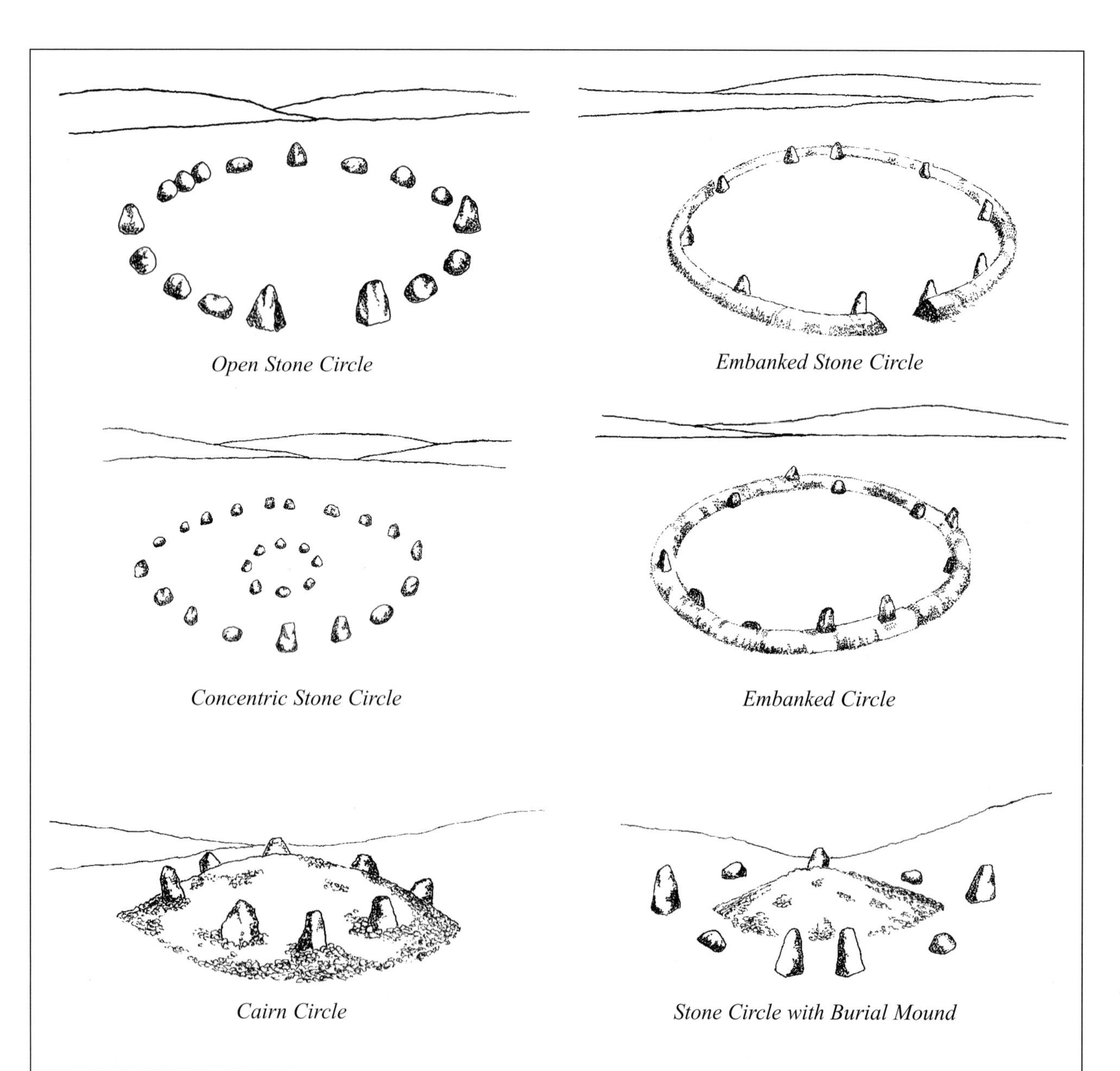

FIGURE 1:
Types of stone circle.

evolved, with the true and the flattened circles being among the earliest, predating the ellipse and egg which are not so numerous.

Thom's contribution to our understanding of megalithic culture has been highly influential. He has forced academia to look with new eyes and to reassess the achievements of the megalithic peoples, but certain aspects of his body of work reflect his own engineering background and here some prudence is needed. Research has shown that it is possible to achieve similar geometries to Thom's categories of design by accident, simply by laying out the circles visually by rule of thumb. Subsequent critiques have shown that all Thom really achieved was to demonstrate that, 'his range of 'standard' shapes provided reasonable fits to the measured data; alternative sets of shapes could be found that seemed to fit the data equally well.' (Ruggles, 1999). Thom's studies have also suggested methods of construction for the circles, using stakes and cords to draw the designs on the ground, while other studies have proposed similar construction techniques using much simpler methods (Curtis, 1988; Cowan, 1988). These considerations introduce a note of caution against accepting any one approach to solving the problems posed by the circle builders – a fact recognised by Thom himself. 'No method of rigid proof can be produced to show that this construction was actually used by the erectors,' he wrote.

Did the ancient surveyors use the same reference points in constructing circles that we impose with our modern geometries? It is interesting to note that of all the known surveys of Castlerigg (identified by Thom as a flattened circle Type A) none agrees as to the position of the centre. Such differences would have a significant effect upon the position of the stones and circle relative to the horizon and this could result in the validity of any research being seriously questioned. Incidentally, because of the problems of classification highlighted by such surveys, the term 'stone ring' as opposed to 'stone circle' has now been deemed a more accurate description of these structures.

Of all geometric forms the circle provides the best representation of the horizon. It provides a means of ordering the landscape, enabling measurement of the horizon. Its circularity mirrors the rim of the horizon, and like a hub it lies at the very centre of the landscape. A large number of stone circles have been shown to have significant stones with properties enabling them to project further into the landscape – calendrical and cardinal trends as well as alignments to certain landscape features. However, not all the stones around the perimeter of a circle do this and the position of many cannot be accounted for. It may be that many of the stones of a circle, besides fulfilling a 'scientific' function, were also symbolically important to the community, because the circles were also places of cultural identity. It might be that any number of commemorations, important occasions for celebration such as anniversaries, births, deaths, coronations and battles would be the criteria which determined the placing of stones around a circle. The stones may appear irregular to us but would have been meaningful to the community to which it belonged. The circles are ritual monuments and mystery was encoded as part of their grand design. The builders were the architects of mystery incorporating occult and sacred traditions which are endemic to other kinds of houses of the holy.

The astronomical orientations of stone circles mark events such as the rising and setting positions of the sun, moon and also the brighter stars at important times. Solar orientations have been found to mark the summer and winter solstices (20-21 June and 21/22 December), and the vernal and autumnal equinoxes (21 March and 23 September). Thom further proposed evidence for a sixteen-month solar calendar with the solstices and equinoxes further divided by the four ancient 'Celtic' festivals of Imbolc, Beltane, Lughnasa and Samhain (Burl, 1988). In

Table I (see page 24) are the declinations and azimuths for this calendar calculated to sea level and a horizon of 0 degrees, for an approximate guide, for the latitude of Castlerigg (Burl, 1988). The movements of the moon are more complex but an understanding of the lunar cycle would have been highly beneficial during the hours of darkness. The moon's 28 day cycle closely resembles that of the solar year with the moon's rising and setting positions following a similar path to that of the sun. The moon completes a full cycle in 18.6 years and has eight limiting directions of rising and setting compared to the sun's four at the solstices (see Fig. 2. page 24). The moon's arc of rising and setting is sometimes wide across the horizon, called the 'major standstill'; when the arc of rising and setting is at its smallest this is the 'minor standstill'. It take the moon 9.3 years to travel from a major to a minor standstill and 18.6 years to complete the cycle. The major standstills every 18.6 years must have been the most impressive of lunar phenomena. At the Northern Major Standstill the moon rises and sets almost due north (at these latitudes) and a fortnight later at the Southern Major Standstill it makes its lowest transit across the sky, reaching its lowest altitude. In the northern hemisphere this lunar phenomenon is more pronounced and in Shetland 'the Moon at its furthest north is almost circumpolar' (Thom, 1973). This remarkable occurrence would surely have attracted the notice of those watching the night sky, even though observations were required over the long period of the lunar cycle. Castlerigg has been shown to be a prime location for observing this event, incorporating three lunar standstill azimuths within its compass (see Castlerigg).

Mountains and hills dominate the Lakeland landscape and many stone circles seem to possess astronomically significant positions in relation to them, although the magnitude of a mountain or hill will obviously cover a broad sector of

Survey of Castlerigg, Alexander Thom, with kind permission of the Royal Commission on the Ancient and Historic Monuments of Scotland.

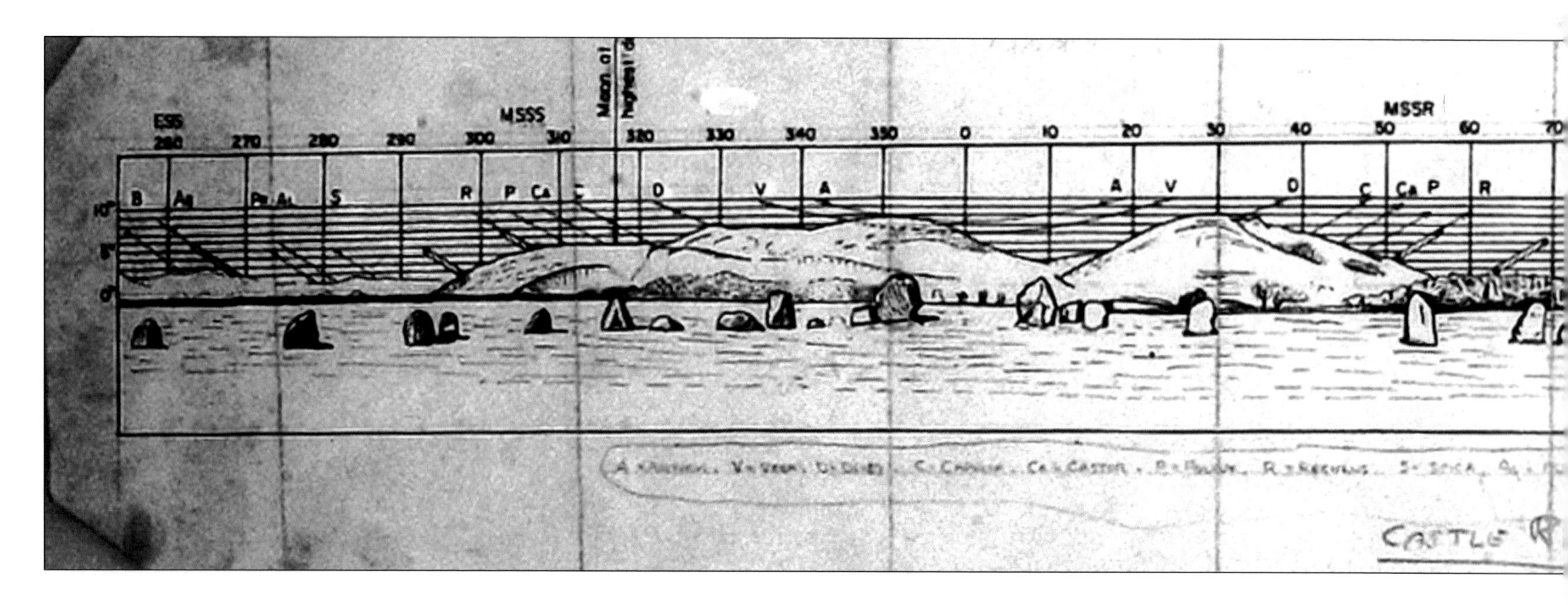

the horizon and a wide range of azimuths. Such celestial 'mountain clocks' have been documented in many other mountainous regions from all seven continents. Just one example, from the Harz mountains in Germany, is an equinoctial alignment which closely resembles the Mayburgh Henge – Blencathra orientation. From the Nebra settlement – a prehistoric hill top enclosure – the sun sets at the equinox behind the Brocken, the highest mountain in the Harz range.

While some circles could serve an astronomical purpose, many can only be regarded as symbolic. Many circles also seem to incorporate the major cardinal points in the lay out of their foundations. It has been said that nowhere in the British Isles are these features more apparent than in the great stone circles of Cumbria (Burl, 1988 and 2000). Some circles, including Castlerigg, Gunnerkeld, Iron Hill, Swinside and thc Beacon, have very definite cardinal trends. Elsewhere such cardinal lines seem to suggest even more impressive calendrical concerns. At Long Meg, a massive boulder to the west is south of true west, as Burl has observed, 'equidistant between the observed winter and summer settings. What looks like cardinal inaccuracy to today's investigator was solar precision to the people who set up the stone' (Burl, 1999).

Thom's surveys have shown that many stone circles had astronomical uses – a multiplicity of orientations to the sun, moon and stars. Archaeo-astronomy has proven to be one of the most contentious issues surrounding the study of stone circles and its validity has often been questioned. For example it could be expected that some alignments would result purely from chance in a circle deploying a large number of standing stones; many circles have produced few if any alignments. However, monuments such as Mayburgh Henge, which has one principal axis of orientation aligned with some

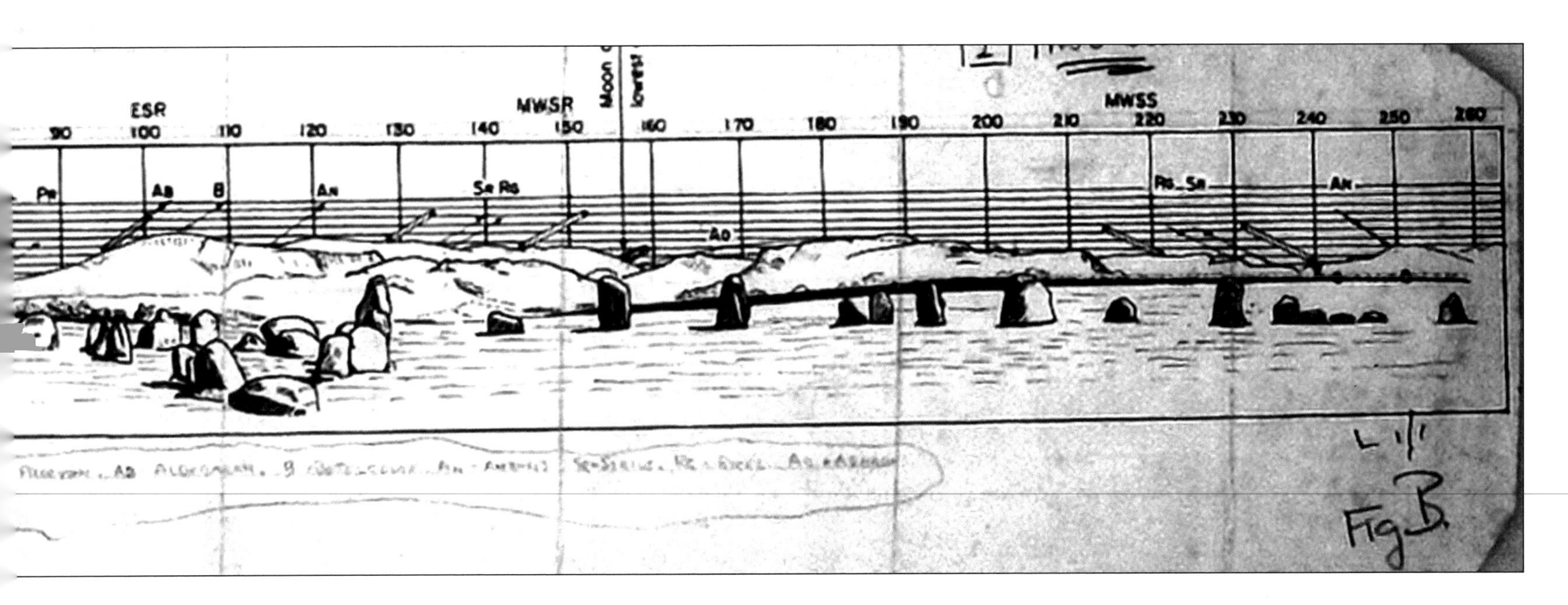

DATE	SUNRISE		SUNSET	
	Declination degrees	Azimuth degrees	Declination degrees	Azimuth degrees
Vernal Equinox, March 21	+0.4	89.4	+0.6	271.0
Beltane, May 1	+16.6	60.6	+16.7	299.8
Summer Solstice, June 21	+23.9	45.6	+23.9	314.4
Lughnasa, August 1	+16.8	60.1	+16.6	299.6
Autumn Equinox, September 23	+0.5	89.1	+0.3	270.6
Samhain, November 1	-16.2	118.9	-16.4	240.5
Winter Solstice, December 21	-23.9	134.4	-23.9	225.6
Imbolc, February 1	-16.3	118.9	-16.2	241.3

TABLE 1: Declinations and Azimuths for the Cumbrian Rings.

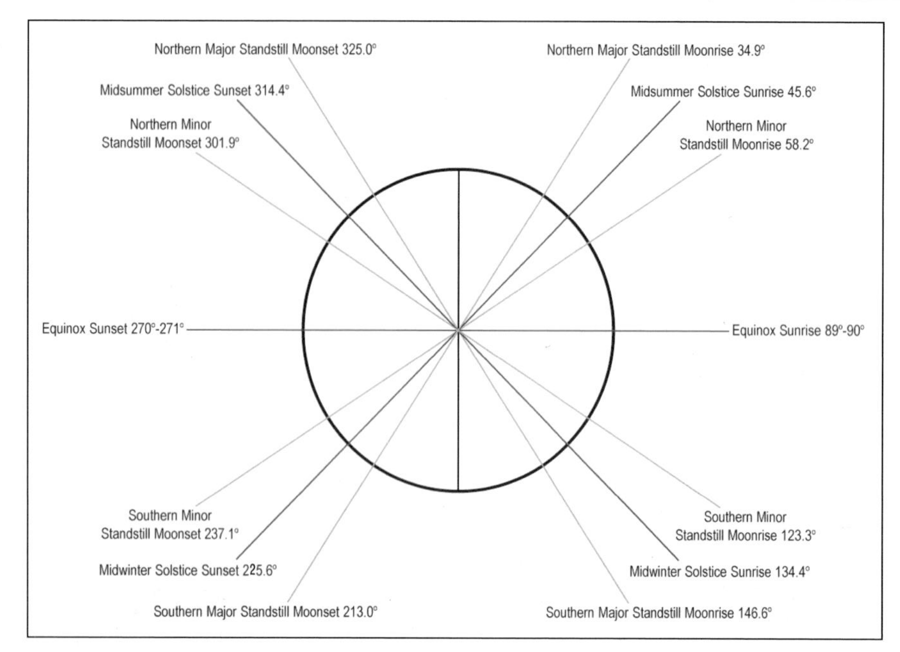

FIGURE 2: The limiting directions of the sun and moon for the latitude of Castlerigg.

Sequence of the setting sun at the equinox on the Saddle of Blencathra at the Mayburgh Henge.

precision, would seem to refute such criticism. The astronomical and cardinal trends exhibited in stone circles may strengthen the suggestion that the circles are linked to the trade in stone axes, because they could provide a barometer to the climatic conditions of the 'factory sites' in a mountain environment. Accessing such sites in the winter months, between the autumn and vernal equinoxes, could have proven a highly dangerous undertaking.

Studies in the 'megalithic sciences' imply that the circle's builders possessed an advanced knowledge of geometry and astronomy, something that academia has been slow to acknowledge. Archaeologists have applied modern values and western logic in trying to understand the societies of the past. Underlying this rationalisation is Zipf's 'Principle of Least Effort', which lies at the foundation of our own materialistic society. As Richard Bradley observes, the 'assumptions that [academics] make are those of the contemporary economy; that goods should be produced with the smallest amount of labour and the greatest potential profit' (Bradley, 2000). This approach has proven problematic when it comes to interpreting certain aspects of the prehistoric past, where the ritual monuments of the megalithic period have often been shown to possess what appear to be more aesthetic and idealistic qualities, totally contrary to the pragmatic considerations of the 'Principle of Least Effort'. One of our most respected and eminent authorities on megalithic history, Aubrey Burl, has written that 'the only known certainties in archaeology are that all archaeologists must die'.

It is clear that stone circles now exist independently of historic time, whereas their study is temporal. Much concerning these ancient places will remain beyond our understanding; indeed this element of mystery is part of their attraction. The once-prevailing materialistic outlook, with its emphasis on measurement, and the use of the pick and trowel to explore the tangible aspects of these ancient sites, is beginning to relinquish its hold, surrendering to more psycho-historical developments. It is now being understood that it is impossible fully to construct and re-establish the past from broken bones, artefacts and remnants of fallen stones. The sheer investment of labour by megalithic builders points to perennial motives which have no objective basis. The meaning of these monuments has proved elusive to the interpretive eye of reason and difficult to quantify and demonstrate. The mystery of these places so often remarked upon was, I suggest, deliberately encoded within them. The permanence of stone was used to express a subliminal spirit. Their foundations were designed to create the very mystery so many seem to experience at these places, often interpreted in an intangible and spiritual light.

More recent explorations are now opening up new fields of research in archaeology with a view to understanding the psychological forces behind the continuing tradition of stone circle construction and location. Archaeology has increasingly become concerned with prehistoric cognition, ideology and phenomenological studies - perspectives where quantifiable interpretations often become difficult and unrealistic. It is clear that stones circles were designed and sited according to aesthetic, visual and emotional responses, qualities which have been described as the 'sensual archaeologies'.

Stukeley's words describing his experience of 'exstatic reverie, which none can describe, and they only can be sensible of it that feel it' at Stonehenge, has a certain resonance. Such lines of enquiry would consider, for example, the impact of a monument on an observer; the visual presence of the monument in the landscape; quality such as the size, shape, colour and composition of the stones; sound sensations; the play of light upon a monument. An infinite index of possible enquiry mapping the prehistoric mind.

Stone circles were amongst the first surviving consciously constructed ceremonial monuments and their

Mayburgh Henge sunrise at the Equinox.

presence is now regarded as integral to a more subliminal landscape imbued with an ancestral mythology. Phenomenological approaches explore the possible symbolic relationships between the monuments and the natural features in the landscape and the celestical skyscape. It considers the landscape as charged with meaning and mythological significance. It is suggested that their location within the landscape took place according to an ancient and established symbolism. Often described as both Druid Circle and Temple, or more progressively as the Kirk, we are reminded how these sites were regarded as spiritual thresholds and places of communion. The stone circle can be seen as a mandala to 'The Great Circle' and as such its symbolic power is strengthened when freed from association. In the past these monuments were vandalised by the hand of man, broken by fire and water and later with dynamite. It may be that they are further vandalised by our own reasoning.

There is a trend for seeing stone circles as beyond the settled landscape, serving as thresholds to a symbolic and ritual landscape, [see note 1, Appendix V]. The land on which they are found is often intermediary, lying between the lowlands of the valleys and the highlands of the fells and mountains, affording views of both. Long Meg and her Daughters is a good example. This circle is located at the head of a valley which leads down to the River Eden, which served as a principal route from the Solway plain to the interior. From this approach Long Meg is positioned on the edge of the plateau, and its location was hidden from view from the valley by the rise of a hill. The valley of the Eden effectively acts as a blindfold to the surrounding landscape which remains unseen until the final approach to the circle. On the ascent to the circle the views gradually open up, revealing magnificent panoramas of the distant Lakeland fells in the west and south west and the backdrop of the Pennines to the east. The views continue to improve, and are given full realisation within the perimeter of the circle. The full circle can be seen to encompass the final rise of the valley, with the stones to the north east at the lower end and those to the south west, including Long Meg, seen against the skyline of the local horizon, the summit of the plateau. On the approach to Long Meg from the lower stones through the centre of the circle the landscape is finally revealed in its totality, and the focus of the circle's orientation is realised when Helvellyn rises above the western portal stones.

This experience of landscape revelation at Long Meg is common in the approach to many stone circles. Ascending necessitates the crossing of a

threshold that lies beyond the inhabited landscape into the region of the ritual. To the megalithic peoples this ritual landscape and its boundary would have been clearly defined. However, later settlement destroyed this boundary, and has also destroyed some of the monuments. Not all is lost, though, for quite often the outline features of the historic landscape have been preserved and the main land forms remain.

The use of the stone circles for interments has further imbued them with a ceremonial and symbolic significance. The stone circle was not used exclusively for burial – they were not used as cemeteries. Often only one or a few interments are found, sometimes referred to as 'foundation sacrifices'. These sites were possibly access points to an Other-world, perceived as an interface between heaven and earth, the living and the dead. Many of the circles still seem to retain a numinous atmosphere, a quality at once magical and other-worldly. Studies have shown that many of the circles are to be found along access routes leading into the heart of the mountains. Mountains have always been regarded as the dwelling places of gods and figure in the origins of many spiritual histories. As Mark Edmonds has suggested, 'elevated places have been prominent in the imaginations of many cultural traditions, in part because they impose themselves so powerfully upon the senses' (Edmonds, 2004). During the approach to such symbolic territory, the unfolding landscape, I suggest, served as a foundation for divine disclosure. Even now these exceptional panoramas have the power to instil within us similarly expansive experiences. It is a landscape our emotions easily understand but which language struggles to define. It is the subliminal landscape of fearful mountains, mists and vapours so beloved of the Romantics. The stone circles, located in a landscape invested with exceptional panoramas and beautiful views, may have been chosen by the builders to mirror the elysium of this Other-world.

These monuments have often been considered in isolation, but increasingly the parameters of archaeology are widening. The relationship between stone circles and their landscape setting is now realised to be crucial. Such geographical features as mountains and hills were places of reverence. Being in a landscape dominated by a central massif of dramatic mountains, stone circles became the focus of that reverence. Indeed many circles do seem to possess careful alignment or orientation, so that the circles and the mountains seem to 'hang together'. The mountains are after all the most prominent and significant features in the landscape. Viewing a circle from the outside also frequently suggests a relationship between the circle and the mountains. The circle often seems to encompass neatly a distant mountain or mountain range. The eye is seemingly drawn through the circle to focus upon the land form. These defining directions seem to cluster around significant trends, suggesting that the circles were positioned relative to the mountains according to both cardinal and astronomical considerations. Some of these considerations were undoubtedly symbolic rather than calendrical. The horizon of this revered landscape was perceived to be circular, mirrored in the circularity of the monuments. Evidence suggests that the monuments were built to influence the ways in which people experienced the landscape according to a pre-ordained cosmology. Anthropological comparison of other societies where the landscape has been invested with both human and sacred significance is helping towards a greater awareness of our own ancestors. The location of the stone circles within the mythologized landscape took place according to an ancient and established code and the mountains were at the centre of this landscape.

Crinkle Crags and Grunting Gill from Pike O'Stickle, Gabriel Blamires

Another aspect of this encoded landscape has possibly found expression in the designs of rock art, our earliest artistic inheritance. Cups, cups surrounded by circles and arcs, cups with grooves, and spirals are amongst the main

This page:Helvelynn - the focus of orientation at Long Meg and her daughters.

Opposite: The Winter Solstice orientation at Long Meg and Her Daughters.

motifs. These are found in two main contexts; on outcrops of rock and on stones in some of the circles. Theories abound as to their nature but any conclusive meaning has so far proven elusive. It has been noted that 'spiral images at Castlerigg and Long Meg and her Daughters face inwards so that they could only have been seen by an audience looking out from these monuments towards the wide views of the encircling hills and mountains… perhaps the images incised into the stone circles were intended to be seen in association with the uplands which feature so prominently in views from these monuments. Not only was the rock art being set against the landscape itself, emphasising a boundary or threshold, but such meanings might feasibly have extended to apply to that topography as well.' (Watson and Bradley in press).

There is an important and substantial cluster of 'rock art' in and around the stone circles of the Eden Valley, suggesting a significant tradition (see Glassonby, Little Meg and Long Meg and her Daughters). Many isolated stones have also been found in the area. Amongst the most important of these are the Honey Pots Farm stone and the Redhills stone. The Honey Pots stone has been described as being 'a very good design, firmly based on the cup and ring tradition' (Beckensall, 2002). Found beside the River Eamont, a tributary of the Eden, this stone is unusual in that its fine design is carved upon whinstone which is hard to work. It is now on display at Tullie House Museum.

The now missing Redhills stone has been called 'one of the finest examples of cup and ring art ever found in Cumbria'. It was rumoured to have once been in the old Penrith Museum, but if so it was lost before the museum relocated. Despite extensive research and an appeal in the local press in the 1980s the stone has proven elusive. However, we are fortunate in possessing a description and a drawing of this stone. It is known to have been a cist cover made of limestone measuring 1.6m (5 feet) by 1m (3.5 feet) with a thickness of 0.2-0.34 m (0.5-1 feet). The

stone's decorated side faced inwards towards the grave, in which was found bones and charcoal. The carvings consisted mainly of numerous cup-shaped hollows, there are two cups with concentric arcs and radial grooves and various interlinking channels.

At present our knowledge of the meaning of these mysterious designs is as lost as the stone. I am persuaded that an acceptance of rock art as symbolic is the only interpretation needed to make their meanings accessible. The nature of their symbolism is abstract and can only be understood intuitively – it evades rational understanding. The circularity of the main designs may be cosmologically symbolic. There is the simulacra of the natural world: the heat-giving orb of the sun, the moon waxing from a void to a complete circle, the stars turning around some invisible fulcrum, the cycle of the seasons and the evidence for cardinal and calendrical functions in the stone circles. Time is experienced as cyclic. A close analogy of this symbolism is the crucifix, which is meaningful on so many levels the whole can never be described. And just as the crucifix is realised in the ground plan of churches and cathedrals, so the circularity of rock art is realised and given full expression in the ground plan of the stone circles. Christopher Tilley has suggested that megalithic architecture was a new constitution of 'cultural markers… used to create a new sense of place… whilst continuing to make reference or lay claim to already established ancestral connections with, and pathways through, the landscape' (Tilley,1994).

To conclude, evidence suggests that stone circles were powerful places of cultural identity. They were spiritual outposts, isolated from normal settlement, along access routes into the mountains, the beginning and end to perilous journeys into those forbidding regions. They were the trading places to which people journeyed from near and far in search of the precious stone which would become the Promethean axe, giving shape to both land and destiny. Evident in the circle's design and construction are the megalithic sciences of geometry, mathematics and astronomy – inherent in many are alignments to calendrical declinations of the sun, moon and stars.

It was these associations which were persuasive in connecting the ancient priesthood of the Druids with the monuments in the minds of the early antiquarians. With the advent of Romanticism this mountain wilderness inhabited by the ruins of druidic temples became revered. All these elements, and the themes of this guide, are present in a painting of the period called 'The Bard', by Thomas Jones, of 1774 (see page 2). The last bard is standing on the edge of a precipice near a withered and blasted oak, contemplating death while escaping the persecution of Edward I's order to destroy the druidic order. He is looking pensively upon a scene which is a composite of all the wisdom of that order, soon to be lost forever. The bard is looking back over the nearby heel stone of the druidic temple of Stonehenge to the last glow of the midwinter setting sun (both deified and worshipped by the priesthood) upon the heights of Snowden. Although this Romantic vision is both geographically and historically inaccurate it is intuitively and spiritually correct. Anthropology has shown that many monuments were regarded as the focus of a land invested with symbolic meaning. They were regarded as thresholds from the temporal world to a liminal place, where contact was made with the supernatural. These ritualised monuments were constructed to connect to a mythologised landscape. They developed out of places which had sacred significance, as liminal locations where metamorphosis of the consciousness was experienced.

Many megalithic monuments have also been shown to possess some significant associations with the surrounding land, suggesting the possibility of just such a mythologised landscape. When Wordsworth tried to fathom the truth behind Long Meg's 'mystic round', his feelings were those we all share. He asks the 'Giant-mother' to speak

Opposite, clockwise, from upper right corner: a sprial and concentric circle rock carving at Little Meg; a cist cover stone from Little Meg; a cup-marked stone from Redhills, Penrith.

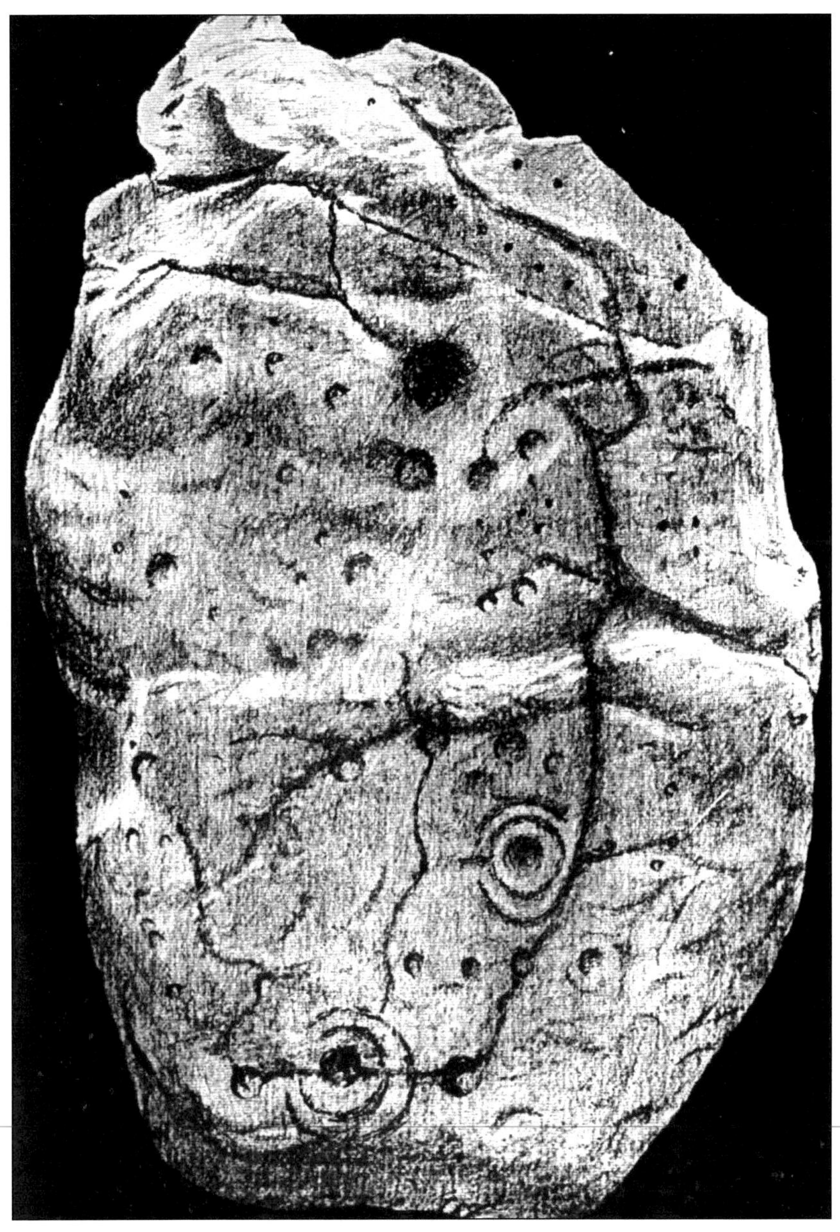

of the 'when, how and wherefore…' We may ask ourselves what relevance these remote antiquities have in our own time. Wordsworth believed that Long Meg was a 'wondrous monument' of the 'inviolable God', and that the quest for an understanding of the 'mystic round' is irrevocably bound to our enlightenment and ability to transcend our own cultural alienation. Conscious of these sentiments and this inheritance, the historic environment is now being assessed and incorporated in management strategies to help conserve their significance. It is hoped that this more integrated approach may help to preserve them from further destruction. These ancient landscapes are still evolving today.

Aquatint print of Mayburgh Henge by T H Fielding, c1822, by kind permission of Penrith Museum

ABOUT THE GUIDE

BEFORE CONSULTING THIS guide in preparation for visiting a monument, there are certain particulars to consider to make the visit safer, more instructive and enjoyable. As in all mountainous areas, the Cumbrian weather is notoriously changeable and each valley can have its own weather system. Although the stone circles are generally sited on lower-lying ground peripheral to the central dome of mountains, they are still close enough to come within their compass and the terrain may sometimes prove hostile. Make sure you are prepared for these conditions with the provision of adequate waterproof clothing and suitable footwear. Before visiting the more isolated stone circles, many of which are found at more exposed elevations, obtain a weather forecast. A local weather bulletin is usually more accurate in mountain environments, and these can be obtained from Tourist Information Centres. In the hills, a strengthening wind can bring a significant wind chill and lowering cloud can mean poor visibility. Although many of the circles are a stroll from the car, some are more remote and may necessitate careful navigation through more inhospitable terrain. Be warned!

The Countryside and Rights of Way Act 2000 (CROW) introduced a statutory right of access to land that has been designated and mapped as 'access land'. This access land is defined as mountain, moor, heath and down (including land over 600m) registered as common land. These new 'Rights to Roam' were introduced in 2004 and implemented in the Lakes and Cumbria in 2005, opening a further 10-15% of marginal land within the county. Many of the stone circles within this guide are to be found on such marginal land, but not all fall within the compass of the new access land. Some stone circles are to be found on enclosed land and some of these will have restricted access; a visit to these will need the permission of the landowner. Although it is a courtesy to seek the permission of the landowner in practise this is not always viable. At short notice a landowner cannot always be found and it must also be an annoyance to a busy farmer to be pestered by callers. Let common sense prevail. In my own experience most landowners are sympathetic to the interest shown in the monuments that occur on their land and have accordingly made access easier by permissive paths and by incorporating stiles into walls. All access land will be shown on the new OS Explorer Maps from 2005; updated information will also be available on the website www.countrysideaccess.gov.uk.

Although the Romantics probably preferred the ruined druidic stones to be clothed in mists and vapours, when that ghost land of the other-world suddenly seems more accessible, the surrounding landscape is integral to our understanding of them. A map and compass are essential equipment for walking in the hills, and will enable a better understanding of the monuments. The stone circles are a focus of the landscape, and a map will help in identifying features of that landscape and the nature of the terrain. The Ordnance Survey Explorer maps OL4, OL5, OL6 and OL7 are highly recommended, and with a few exceptions, cover all of the circles mentioned in this guide.

In a few instances some of the circles have been particularly difficult to locate. To improve on this, all locational references in the guide have been obtained from the centre of the circle by GPS, subject to the usual variation in accuracy. I have also given compass bearings as a directional aid. The circle is the perfect shape for the ascertaining of direction, and a stone circle functions as a primitive compass. The stones of a circle tend to divide the horizon, and a compass will give their directions. The stone circle plans are an abstract isolated from the landscape. Using a compass with the plans given in the guide, orientate the plan to the circle and the landscape. If a compass is not available simply use the sides of the page to represent the cardinal points, with true north to the top of the page. Bear in mind that stone circles were located with reference to the more constant celestial sky and the permanence of the landscape and not the magnetic variation of the compass. Relating the circle to the horizon enables some spatial awareness of the landscape, helping to identify any calendrical, cardinal or other trends present.

Aaron Watson wrote, 'the conventions by which monuments have been routinely recorded and published perpetuate a view of the past that is dependent upon two dimensional imagery, black and white text, highly stylised illustrations and photographic plates. Expressed in this way, monuments from the past are rendered static and lifeless, devoid of sensory experience, movement, change and transition. This results in disembodied perspectives whose importance ultimately exceeds that of experiencing the monuments themselves.' (Watson, 2004a).

These databases cannot harness the dynamic of the landscape. The disciplines that quantify the archaeological record fail to convey the atmospheres of the land. It is the ambition of this guide to address this bias. The concluding sentence in *The Stone Circles of Cumbria* by Waterhouse, that, 'whatever the original uses of the circles, they now have, to my mind, one particular purpose – they provide very worthwhile objectives for excursions in the hills of Cumbria' (Waterhouse, 1985), marked one beginning of this guide. While acknowledging Waterhouse's achievement, this guide is informed by new perspectives from archaeology. It is tempered by a different vision that will further an understanding of these monuments by considering the landscape in which they are located. The dynamic of location is crucial to this study, and may offer insights into monuments which have suffered varying degrees of destruction.

Each site entry in the guide is given the necessary information to aid location, but on arrival the process of engagement with the monument and its landscape begins. I have visited all these sites in contrasting weathers, and these have a profound effect upon the atmosphere of a place and our own experience. A stone circle washed with mists and vapours can generate feelings of disquiet and unease, in total contrast to the same circle seen under blue skies and warm summer sunshine. 'It seems that the 'true' view prioritised by the archaeologist is one that is not distorted by atmospherics, thereby denying the dynamic ever-changing experience of the observer who dwells in the world. Indeed, archaeologists seldom invest time or resources in order to engage with places in contrasting weathers, seasons, or different times of day or night, and it is equally rare for this diversity to be conveyed in published reports' (Watson, 2004c).

Having already mentioned the 'Principle of Least Effort' and its negative effect upon the perception of the prehistoric past I must now confess to having applied exactly this principle to this guide. The directions given follow the quickest and most convenient routes, first to the nearest possible location by car, before continuing on foot. This very approach can destroy our spatial and sensual engagement with the land, resulting in an alienation from the environment. The people who built the stone circles moved to and from them by walking, and walking is integral to developing an understanding of the landscape. Walking intimately engages us with our surroundings. I am persuaded that it is only possible to gain some understanding of these monuments and the historic landscape by moving as those who built them did.

In recent studies, the possible trade routes from the axe 'factory' sites in the mountains to the stone circles and the settlement sites of the lower fells and the coastal plain were traced from associated finds of flakes and rough-outs. It was found that many of the tracks coincided with routes that are still used by those walking the fells. Remember Tilley's

Long Meg and her Daughters. Lithograph reproduced with kind permission of the George Hotel, Penrith.

observation that megalithic architecture was a new constitution which continued to 'make reference or lay claim to already established ancestral connections with, and pathways through, the landscape.' It would seem that these pathways are still an ancestral reference point and an aid in interpreting the meaning of the landscape.

Although the first visit to a stone circle is likely to be the most memorable, the intrinsic qualities of a location will only be understood through frequent visits. Visiting at differing times of day and in different seasons allows one to experience the land in all its many moods and atmospheres. Circle the monument from a distance, and view it from varying angles. If an association is suggested between stone circle, hill or mountain, then, time permitting, journey to that place to experience the engagement, even though the understanding is likely to be sensory. All this will slowly help to develop a sensual engagement with the land and location – the spirit of the place. Remember, the approach given in the guide will almost certainly be governed by the modern landscape and may not necessarily be that used by those who first built the stone circle. Walking is essential to this perception; no other means of movement effectively induces the spirit of contemplation regarding our relationship with the land.

It is no coincidence that this aesthetic of walking was rediscovered and refined by the Romantics as an act of

Pike O'Stickle buttresses and south scree from The Band, Gabriel Blamires.

culture in this very landscape. In an essay called *Wordsworth in the Tropics*, Aldous Huxley noted that 'For good Wordsworthians… a walk in the country is the equivalent of going to church, a tour through Westmorland is as good as a pilgrimage to Jerusalem.' Wordsworth described his own meditations on seeing Long Meg and her Daughters for the first time, on just such a walk:

Speak Giant-mother! Tell it to the Morn,
While she dispels the cumbrous shades of night;
Let the Moon hear, emerging from a cloud,
When, how and wherefore, rose on British ground
That wondrous Monument… William Wordsworth, 1822

The stone circle is both construct and symbol, the circle the most enduring of all designs. It is measurable and yet infinite. Its form a 'mystic round', and the mystery of 'that wondrous monument' remains assured and will endure. The stone-breakers may have had some satisfaction but the stone circle will remain unbroken by any brief concerning their interpretation. The 'Giant-mother' is whispering.

Castlerigg stone circle, from an early 20th century postcard.

Index to the Stone Circles

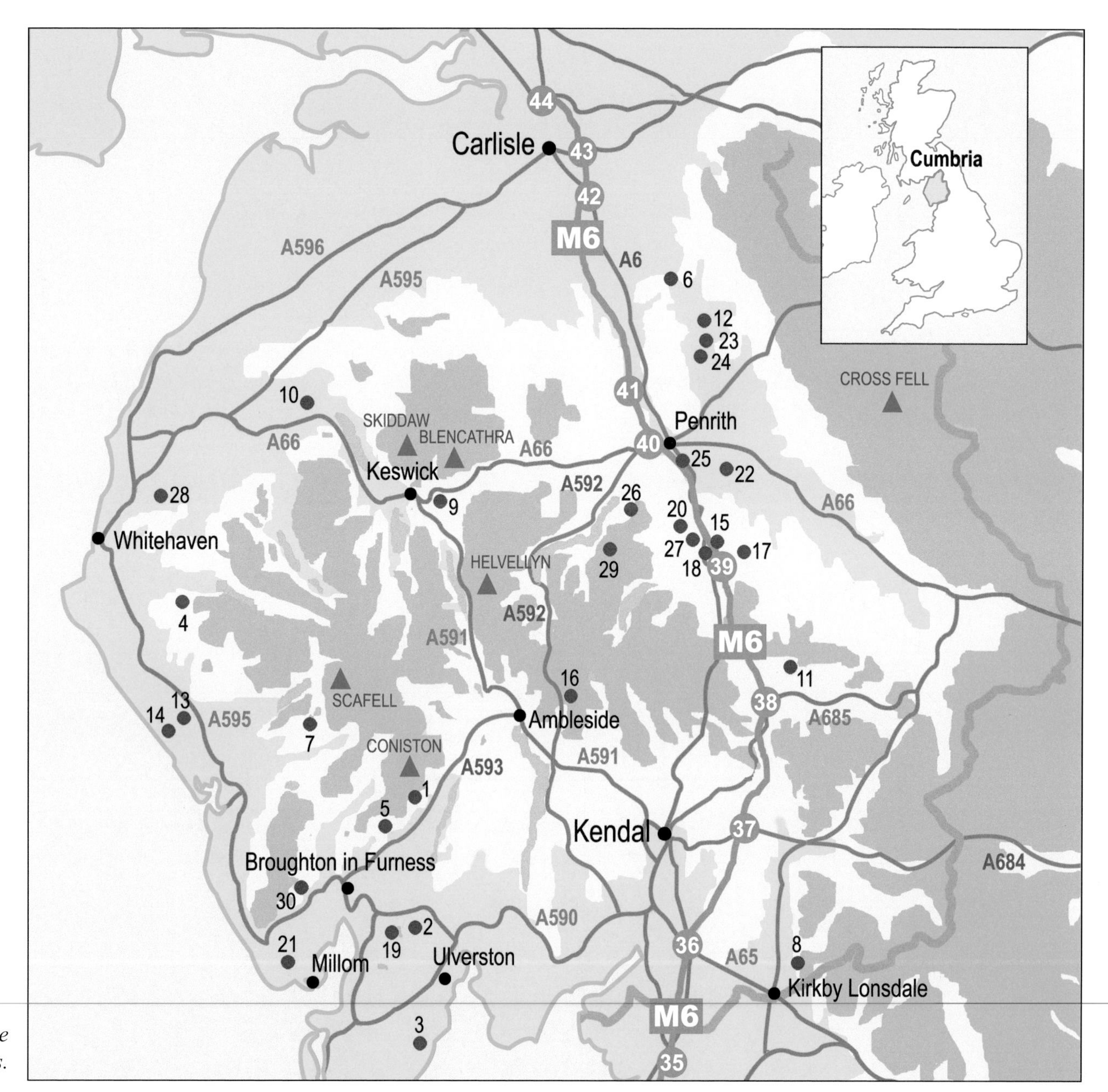

Map of Cumbria showing the main stone circle sites.

1. BANNISIDE

Banniside from the west.

GRID REF: SD 2846 9670.

ELEVATION:
249m (817ft).

MAP: OS Explorer (1:25000) OL6; OS Landranger (1:50000) 97.

LOCATION:
Latitude N 54. 21.648; Longitude WO 03. 06.142: 2km (1.25 miles) WSW of Coniston.

PARKING: Coniston Station car park in Old Furness Road (left off Station Road) or 1.1km (0.7m) distant at the end of the metalled lane leading to Walna Scar Road – Old Man of Coniston.

WALKING DISTANCE:
2.26km (1.4m) from Coniston, 711m (0.4m) from car park before Walna Scar Road.

TERRAIN: Rugged quarry lane, rough pathless moorland, marsh.

DESCRIPTION:
BANNISIDE CIRCLE is a low embankment of stones on a raised bank on the northern edge of a marsh in a shallow valley. The bank of stones has an average width of 3.5m (11.4ft) and reaches a maximum height of 1.2m (3.9ft). The embankment was faced on the inside by a continuous ring of small close fitting slabs with a diameter of 14.6m (47.9ft) NE to SW and 12.8m (41.9ft) transversely. The monument was built upon an artificially levelled platform on the slope of a hill. The present slabs to the WSW have been re-erected after excavation and have the appearance of a set of teeth.

From the true centre of the circle there is a large boulder to the SW which, it has been suggested, may have already been in situ and incorporated as the foundation stone of the circle. A stone to the NW aligns on the summit of Coniston Old Man. Banniside seems to have been located with some significance for the solstice; from the centre of the circle a large stone 57.9m (190ft) to the NE marks the approximate position of the midsummer solstice sunrise and the sun sets on the western edge of the summit of Coniston Old Man; at the winter solstice the sun sets on Bleaberry Haws (see Bleaberry Haws). Just south of the monument is an earthwork which has been interpreted as a 'possible oval mound, some 7m x 4m (22.9ft x 13.1ft)', with its long axis in alignment.

The Banniside Circle was excavated in 1909 and in the raised central area just E of the centre was found an unusual biconical urn containing bone-ash, charcoal and a piece of white quartz spar; this is thought to be the primary burial. A collared urn was found to the N which contained bone-ash and fragments thought to be the skull of a female, a smaller pygmy urn lay on top of the ash which contained the cremated remains of a child. There is a possibility that this was the burial of both a mother and child. The urns date the circle to the early Bronze Age. Finds from the excavation are on display in the Ruskin Museum in Coniston. The circle is dominated by the massive southern aspect of the Old Man of Coniston to the NW.

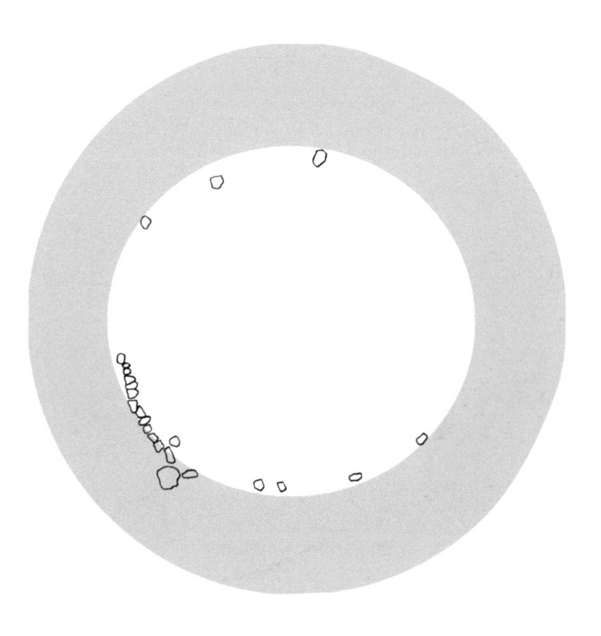

DETAILED DIRECTIONS:
In Coniston, S of Church Bridge turn up Station Road which soon narrows to a lane leading to Walna Scar Road. At the furthest car park continue along Walna Scar for a short distance - 0.4km (0.26m). Here before arriving at a quarry track to the right, a broad grassy track with some sedge grass and marsh leads downhill for about 200m (670ft) to the circle. Banniside stone circle can be seen to the SE on the edge of a marsh.

FURTHER READING:

Collingwood, W.G, *An Exploration of the Circle on Banniside Moor, Coniston*, TCWAAS, Volume 10, 1910.

2. The Beacon

The Beacon looking towards the Coniston Fells.

GRID REF: SD 2800 8423.

ELEVATION: 135m (443ft).

MAP: OS Explorer (1:25000) OL6; OS Landranger (1:50000) 97.

LOCATION: Latitude N 54. 14.923; Longitude WO 03. 06.389: 6km (3.7m) N of Ulverston – 1km (0.6m) SE of Gawthwaite.

PARKING: In vicinity of Knapperthaw Farm – restricted.

WALKING DISTANCE: 0.5km (0.3m).

TERRAIN: Pasture.

DESCRIPTION:

THE CIRCLE is marked as an enclosure on maps but is more accurately described as an embanked stone circle. The presence of the circle seems to have dictated the pattern of the surrounding enclosure. The approach from the S slopes gently down to the enclosure, located on ground which levels before dropping to the N. The levelling of the inner area of the enclosure has been achieved by embanking, creating the steep drop to the N and giving the effect of a platform, reminiscent of Casterton.

There is some semblance of an entrance in the SSW, from which direction the enclosure is approached – possibly the remains of an ancient way. The site is located to the SW of Lowick Common and takes its name from Lowick Beacon, which dominates the eastern horizon. There are valleys to the N and W, giving extensive views towards the Coniston fells and the southern end of the lake. Coniston Old Man is directly N from the centre of the enclosure. This mountain range seems to be the main aspect and focus of the Beacon; the impression is one of an auditorium of mountains.

The enclosure is a bank of earth and stones which surround a level inner area, with a diameter of around 27m (88.5ft) and a height of approximately 0.4m (1.3ft). The bank is lined with stones although very few are visible – just small sections to the NW and SE. The bank in the northern sector is poorly defined in contrast to the SE where it is most evident. The Beacon is mainly an earthwork. From a distance its green banks blend with the surrounding pasture, making it difficult to discern. Although it bears some resemblance to other embanked circles where evidence of interment has been found, and some of the stones inside the circle suggest the existence of an inner structure, possibly a cairn, there is no record of any find associated with the monument. It has some similarity to the Banniside circle beneath Coniston Old Man, approximately 12km (7.4m) to the N, and so may be tentatively dated to the early Bronze Age.

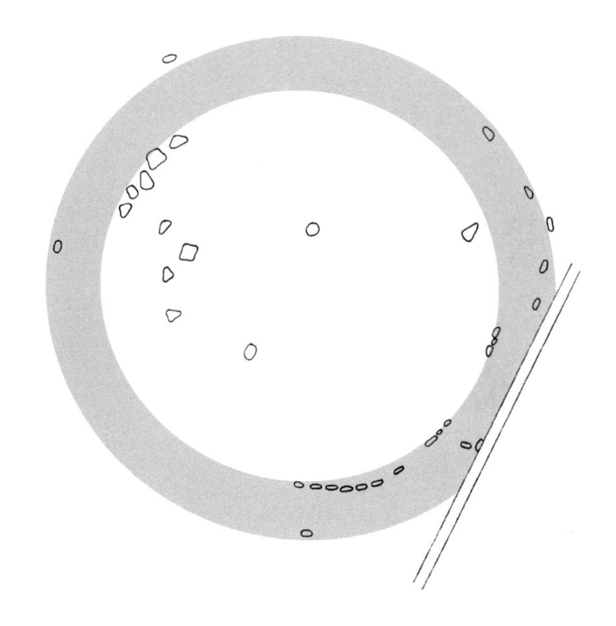

DETAILED DIRECTIONS:

Just W of Gawthwaite turn off the A5092, along the B5281; after 1.6km (1m) turn left at the first road marked 'Coniston 10½' and then take the first right to the farm. Go through the gated entrance E of the farmhouse through the farm yard and through the two gates ahead. Then bear left along the rutted track following the dry stone wall; this leads to a gate at the top of the field (do not take the clearer track on the right). From the gate bear right in a NE direction uphill towards the trees, then follow the wall along to the gate to the right of the tree enclosure. Go through the gate to a broad band of pasture between two walls. The circle can be seen in the foreground spanning the breadth between the walls where the tree enclosure ends. Although on common land there is no right of way to the circle and permission is needed from the farm.

3. Birkrigg Common - The Druid Circle

Birkrigg from the north west.

GRID REF:
SD 2923 7396.

ELEVATION:
70m (230ft).

MAP: OS Explorer (1:25000) OL6; OS Landranger (1:50000) 97.

LOCATION:
Latitude N 54.09.398; Longitude WO 03.05.106: 5km (3.1m) S of Ulverston, 0.75km (0.5m) SW of Bardsea.

PARKING:
On the A5087 at Sea Wood on the Furness peninsula. Just opposite is the lane to Sunbrick, which leads to Birkrigg Common.

WALKING DISTANCE:
2km (1.25m).

TERRAIN:
Country lane, grassy downland with clear paths.

DESCRIPTION:
THE STONE circle is located on the SE side of Birkrigg Common, which is designated an area of Limestone Pavement. Birkrigg Common is the highest point in a region of low limestone hills. The circle overlooks the village of Bardsea to the NE, and the farmstead of Sunbrick, which can be seen immediately to the W. The importance of this common in prehistoric times is evident from the many bronze age tumuli and other earthworks which are to be found in the vicinity.

The circle is located on a gentle slope enclosed by higher land from the SW to the N. The aspect from the N through to the S is open with lovely views of the Ulverston estuary and the Morecambe Bay sands. The circle comprises of two nearly concentric stone rings, with diameters of 8.5m (28ft) and 24m (79ft). The circles are closer to the N. It was noted in the report of the later 1921 excavation that 'although no standard of measurement by early man is known… the inner circle's diameter averages 27 feet… several stones of the outer circle were found to be 27 feet apart.'

The inner circle is the more clearly defined with twelve stones of mostly regular height; two are just visible above the ground

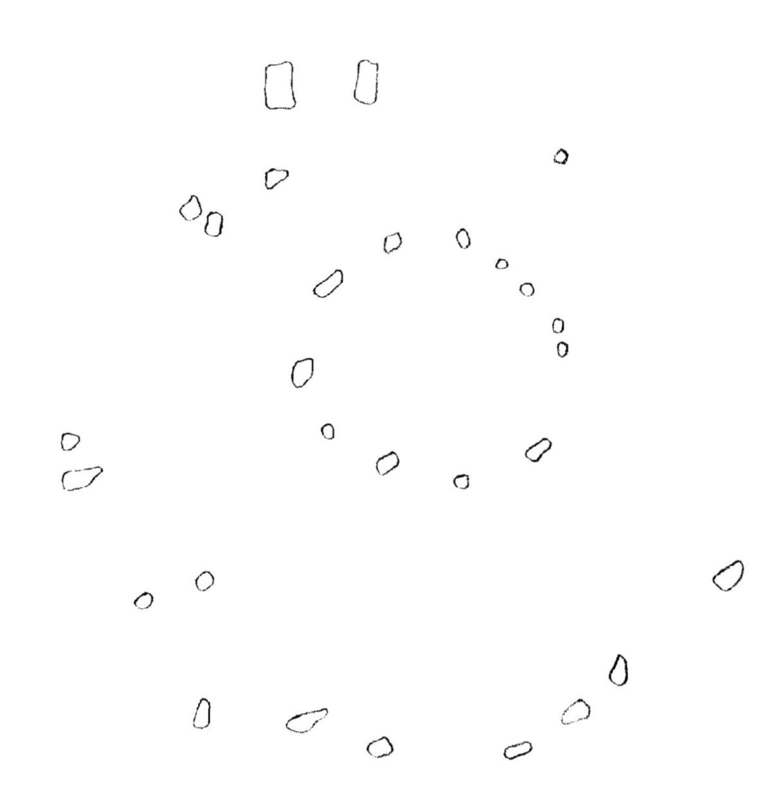

DETAILED DIRECTIONS:
From Ulverston follow the A5087 for Bardsea and continue for approximately 6km (3.7m) to Sea Wood. Take the lane opposite Sea Wood to Sunbrick and Birkrigg Common shortly crossing a cattle grid. The lane climbs steadily uphill for approximately 0.5km (0.3m) past a quarried area on the right. Immediately after the quarry take the path to the right heading NNW towards the corner of a dry stone wall. From here the circle is just visible to the NNW about 90m (300ft) distant and can be hidden by bracken in the summer months.

while the taller stones are near 1m (3.3ft). The stones are of local Carboniferous limestone and are severely eroded by weathering. The stones gleam white in sunlight, contrasting boldly with the surrounding grassland.

The outer ring is not so conspicuous or regular, with approximately twenty low-lying stones, many of which are hidden by bracken, and a section in the NE is incomplete. During excavation in 1911 it was ascertained that both the inner and outer circles were paved with cobbles, the pavement ending at the outer circle. Beneath this pavement, separated by a thin layer of soil, was found another pavement of similar character to the upper one. The cobbles consisted of a stone known as 'blue rag' which is not of local origin and must have been brought from a distance.

Beneath the lower pavement of the inner circle were found the remains of five cremations. The most important of these finds was an inverted urn containing earth, charcoal and calcined bones. The collared urn, dating to the early Bronze Age, had a height of 13.4cm (5.2in) and a diameter across the rim of 12.6cm (4.9in), having a capacity of approximately 1.6 pints. It was made of coarse clay decorated with a twisted cord on the outside, and had two incised lines ornamenting the rim around the lip of the vessel. The central area seems to have been in use over a long period of time because the pit from where the urn was recovered had impacted on an earlier one.

FURTHER READING:

Barnes, F, *Prehistoric Pottery from Furness*, TCWAAS, Volume 70, 1970.

Elsworth, Daniel W., *An early depiction of the Druid's Circle at Birkrigg,* TCWAAS, Volume VI, 2006.

Gelderd, G and Dobson, J, *Report on the Excavations carried out at the 'Druid's Circle' on Birkrigg in the Parish of Urswick, September, 1911*, TCWAAS, Volume 12, 1912.

Gelderd, G, *Report on the further excavations carried out at the 'Druid's Circles,' on Birkrigg in the Parish of Urswick*, TCWAAS, Volume 22, 1922

Birkrigg from the south west.

4. Blakeley Raise

Blakeley Raise from the east.

GRID REF:
NY 0601 1403.

ELEVATION:
225m (738ft).

MAP: OS Explorer (1:25000) OL4: OS Landranger (1:50000) 89.

LOCATION:
Latitude 54.30.771; Longitude 03.27.197: 4km (2.5m) E of Cleator Moor, 2.5km (1.5m) S of Ennerdale Bridge.

PARKING:
Roadside grass verge.

WALKING DISTANCE:
Negligible.

TERRAIN:
High moorland road, sedge and tussock grass, some marsh.

DESCRIPTION:

BLAKELEY RAISE is located on the westerly edge of a moorland wilderness with an impressive outlook. The circle takes its name from the summit of Blakeley Raise to the E, but it is also known locally as the Kinniside stone circle. The land to the W falls away with views of Whitehaven and the coast. On a clear day the Isle of Man can be seen and also the distant hills of Dumfries and Galloway to the N.

The circle is approximately 16.6m (54.5ft) in diameter and consists of eleven regularly spaced stones some 4.3m (14ft) apart, in a perfect circle surrounding a low tumulus about 5m (16.4ft) in diameter. From the centre of the circle the saddle of Grike dominates the local skyline at an elevation of 488m (1,601ft) to the E at 95°, where the sun rises at the equinox. In a survey of the circle Thom has shown that an alignment from the tallest stone to the SE, through the centre of the circle to the distant Screel Hill in Dumfrieshire to the NW, marks the setting position of the moon at the Northern Major Standstill.

There is no record of an internment or other artefacts having been found within the mound or circle, so no reliable date can be given. However, a chronological analysis of its features suggest a date of circa 2500-2000BC, the early Bronze Age. An inventory for Cumberland reports that the circle originally consisted of thirteen stones, eight of which were taken away to make a gateway.

They were replaced in their original position in 1925 in a partial restoration, and there has been some criticism concerning the accuracy of this work. During the restoration work the stones were set in concrete. They are all granite except two, which are a dark igneous rock. The stones are comparatively tall compared to the diameter of the circle. The two tallest stones, approximately 1m (3.3ft) in height, are to the S of the circle, possibly marking an entrance.

It seems that another stone circle was located in an 'infield' of the nearby Standing Stones Farm to the SW. It was reported to the Ordnance Survey in 1967, where it is stated that the stones were removed in the 18th century for gateposts. The author of the report seems to suggest that some of the stones from this circle were re-erected at Blakeley Raise. But there may be some confusion over the two very different locations, one an 'infield' and Blakeley Raise on moorland.

DETAILED DIRECTIONS:
Take the Calder Bridge/Gosforth fell-side road, the stone circle is clearly visible a few metres to the E of the road.

FURTHER READING:

Clare, T, *Some Cumbrian Stones Circles in Perspective*, TCWAAS, Volume 75, 1975.
Fair, M.C, *Standing Stones. Proceedings 410*, TCWAAS, Volume 28, 1928.

5. Bleaberry Haws

Bleaberry Haws from the south.

GRID REF:
SD 2642 9465.

ELEVATION:
325m (1066ft).

MAP: OS Explorer (1:25000) OL6: OS Landranger (1:50000) 97.

LOCATION:
Latitude N 54.20.531; Longitude WO 03.08.003: 4.75km (2.9m) SW of Coniston, 1.9km (1.2m) WNW of Torver.

PARKING:
At Torver Village Hall.

WALKING DISTANCE:
3km (1.8m).

TERRAIN:
Fellside footpath, rough stone track, some marsh.

DETAILED DIRECTIONS:
Pass the Parish Church of St.Luke and the Church House Inn, then take the public footpath to the side of the Wilson Arms. After 0.3km (0.2m) a gate straight ahead gives access uphill to the front of High Park Cottage. Continue around the house to a second gate giving access to a broad path between two walls in the midst of a plantation. After a third gate the path bears right, continuing uphill along a rough stone track. At a fourth gate follow the path uphill along the line of the wall which eventually leads to a stile giving access to the open fell with Bleaberry Haws due W, the summit cairn clearly visible. Avoid taking the direct route which has extensive areas of bog and marsh and instead follow the path to higher, drier ground and onto the northern shoulder of the fell.

DESCRIPTION:

THE CIRCLE of Bleaberry Haws is located 152.4m (500ft) WSW of the summit cairn, one of many on the ridge. The circle is seldom visited, having very little presence owing to its diminutive size, but it has a magnificent location, marred only by the eyesore of the nearby Broughton Moor Slate Quarry to the SW. To the S are extensive views of the Duddon Sands and the Lakeland Penninsulas. Also to the S is the wind farm on Lowick High Common which marks the location of the Kirk stone circle. To the N is the magnificent southern aspect of Buck Pike, Dow Crag and the Old Man of Coniston.

In common with many other stone circles in Cumbria, which are often cardinally related to significant landforms, mostly hills and mountains, Bleaberry Haws is directly S of Dow Crag. Although Coniston Old Man is higher, Dow Crag appears to be higher from Bleaberry Haws. The circle is located on a small level area just below the summit of Bleaberry Haws, and this has undoubtedly been a factor determining the size of the ring. The circle consists of seven small stones of elliptical shape with axes 4.7m (15.4ft) NE-SW and 3.7m (12.1ft).

There is some doubt as to the nature of the circle because of a lack of detail concerning the extent and finds of an excavation which took place in the late nineteenth century. The main feature reported was the discovery of a rough pavement of cobble stones which was found at a depth of from two to three feet (60 to 90cm), resting on natural rock. A similar pavement was discovered during the excavation of the more impressive Druid Circle at Birkrigg just 17.5km (10.8m) to the S (see Birkrigg).

The whole area is rich in archaeological remains, all likely dating to the same period. An ancient earthwork described as an entrenchment crosses the area commencing at a group of cairns at Green Rigg Bank, over the summit of Banks, and crossing the valley before ascending the summit of Bleaberry Haws. Along its length are a number of cairns to be found in close proximity. Many of these cairns are found around the lower slopes of Bleaberry Haws and one is given the distinction of being located on the summit just a short distance to the NE of the circle.

The larger cairns are lettered in the archaeological report; of these cairns B (SD 2673 9448) and C (SD 2678 9442) to the SE are in alignment with the summit cairn E (SD 2656 9471). Many of the cairns have evidence of interment in keeping with a Bronze Age date, and the chronological traits of Bleaberry would suggest a similar date. From Banniside, just 2.7km (1.6m) to the NE (see Banniside), the midwinter solstice sun sets on Bleaberry Haws, and this may be why so many cairns are to be found in the vicinity of the hill. The small size of the stones in the circle on Bleaberry Haws suggests that it may have been one of the last rings to be built.

FURTHER READING:

Cowper, H.S, *Some Prehistoric Remains in North Lonsdale*, TCWAAS (Old Series), Volume 9, 1888.

Cowper, H.S, *The Ancient Settlements, Cemeteries and Earthworks of Furness*, Archaeologia, Volume 53, 1853.

Bleaberry Haws from the north.

6. Broomrigg

Broomrigg A.

GRID REF:
Broomrigg A NY 5482 4668;
Broomrigg B NY 5485 4659;
Broomrigg C NY 5481 4646;
Broomrigg D NY 5496 4658.

ELEVATION:
Broomrigg A 191m (627ft);
Broomrigg B 190m (623ft);
Broomrigg C 190m (623ft);
Broomrigg D 190m (623.3ft).

MAP: OS Explorer (1:25000) OL5; OS Landranger (1:50000) 86.

LOCATION:
Broomrigg A Latitude N 54.48.775; Longitude WO 02.42.269.
Broomrigg B Latitude N 54.48.737; Longitude WO 02.42.236.
Broomrigg C Latitude N 54.48.661; Longitude WO 02.42.270.
Broomrigg D Latitude N 54.48.722; Longitude WO 02.42.133.
17km (10.5m) N of Penrith, 1km (0.5m) E of Ainstable.

PARKING:
Restricted, at entrance to forest track.

WALKING DISTANCE:
Broomrigg B – 0.7km (0.4m);
Broomrigg A, D & C – 0.8km (0.5m).

TERRAIN:
Woodland track, rough pathless forest, some marsh

DESCRIPTION:

BROOMRIGG IS a fascinating complex of archaeological sites on a low hill, with the Pennines to the E and the Eden valley to the W. Broomrigg is the northern-most site of a rich megalithic complex located on the same ridge, including Long Meg, Little Meg, and Glassonby, all running parallel with the Pennines.

Also on the same ridge, just N of Broomrigg, was the great circle of Grey Yauds, described as consisting of 88 large stones forming an almost perfect circle 47.5m (156ft) in diameter. Only a large outlier to the circle now survives. The once-panoramic views from the NE to the S over the Pennines were extensive, but the Broomrigg sites are now isolated from the surrounding landscape by a dense plantation. The tall canopy of trees effectively blankets both light and sound. A heavy, laden silence pervades the forest broken only by bird-song, and the archaeological sites are lost amongst the trees. Broomrigg makes one profoundly aware that these circles were sited in reference to the landscape, purposefully located to be intergral with the surrounding land, and without it something of their overall sense and meaning is lost.

All the sites are marked by red painted wooden stakes, and when the light is good these can be seen scattered throughout the forest. The circles were named Broomrigg A,B,C & D after the first survey of the site in 1930s. Broomrigg B is the first circle seen, just left of the track and S of the wall. Broomrigg B is central to the other three circles, all of which would once have been visible from here. Broomrigg B is a cairn circle and is the smallest of the four circles with a diameter of 3.4m (11ft).

There are four surviving stones out of an original seven, all sandstone, surrounding the central cairn. In the centre of the cairn was a conical-

Broomrigg A

DETAILED DIRECTIONS:
Take the turning for Newbiggin and Croglin approximately 1km (0.6m) SE of Ainstable on the Ainstable – Kirkoswald road. Shortly after passing the turn for 'The Harras' on the left there is a forest track on the right with a double gated entrance. This track soon leads past the first of the archaeological sites to the right of the track and a little further on a second site is also passed on the right. These sites are marked by wooden stakes painted red. Eventually a dry stone wall is reached which continues across the track N to S. This is where all four stone circles are to be found.

Broomrigg B

shaped pit which was lined with stones, giving 'the impression of having been constructed to hold a cinerary urn.'

A remarkable object was found amongst the stones of the cairn during excavation, a rounded block of sandstone with a faint carving bearing some resemblance to a lozenge divided into quarters. The design has been described as skilfully executed. However, the cairn has obviously been tampered with in the past, when it was opened and its contents robbed, so it cannot be known for certain if this carving belongs to the Bronze Age, contemporary with the cairn. It does bear some resemblance to other lozenge motifs known from other megalithic monuments.

Following the line of the wall Broomrigg A soon comes into sight some 100m (330ft) to the NNW. This circle is presumed, by comparison with the others, to be the earliest of the Broomrigg complex. Broomrigg A is also the largest of the circles; the stones of the northern arc still survive, giving an approximate diameter of 55m (180ft). The larger stones are of local sandstone and none stand above 0.9m (3ft) in height; some of the smaller stones are of granite. During excavation in 1950 some of the sockets of the missing stones were found set about 20-22cm (8-9in) into the ground, 'carefully made and packed with small stones.' Evidence of a possible avenue of stones is to be seen to the NW of the circle. The easterly section of the circle has been overlaid by the wall, which uses one of the stones in its foundation.

Broomrigg C is 150m (500ft) SSW of Broomrigg B, on the other side of the forest track beyond a slight rise. For the sharp-eyed the red stakes are just visible to the right of the track in the distance on the approach to Broomrigg B, but cannot be seen from the latter. Broomrigg C is located within a clearing and is the most defined of the group, having fourteen stones with an approximate diameter of 16m (52ft). The stones are a mixture of sandstone and granite, varying in height from 35.5cm-1.2m (1ft 2in-4ft). The stones appear to be fairly evenly spaced, except for those in the SW sector which are closer set.

The excavation showed that there was no central burial, but several interments were found, all positioned on the perimeter of the circle. The arc of closely-set stones in the SW of the circle did not seem to synchronise with the arc of the larger circle. Excavation showed that the close-set arc of stones belonged to the primary interment, a cairn with a diameter of 4.2m (14ft) surrounded by a small circle of stones, possibly dating to the early Bronze Age. Its NW perimeter was central to the larger and later circle built to accommodate further burials in the middle Bronze Age.

The cist of the primary cairn was found to be empty but two deposits of bones were found crushed together beneath three of the stones identified as belonging to the cairn; these are thought to have been a 'foundation sacrifice.' The other more notable finds from the larger circle came from the SE quadrant where several cremation burials were found. The most notable of these were a large cinerary urn and a pygmy urn which was found nearby. The red stakes of Broomrigg D can be seen just S of E from Broomrigg B to the right of the track and E of the wall, and also in a clearing. Broomrigg D is an irregular and wrecked circle of fallen stones. Only five large stones are now prominent in the centre of the circle, which has an approximate diameter of 5.5m (18ft) by 4.5m (14ft). No trace of a cairn or interment was found during excavation in 1960, only a few pieces of pottery and some worked flakes of flint.

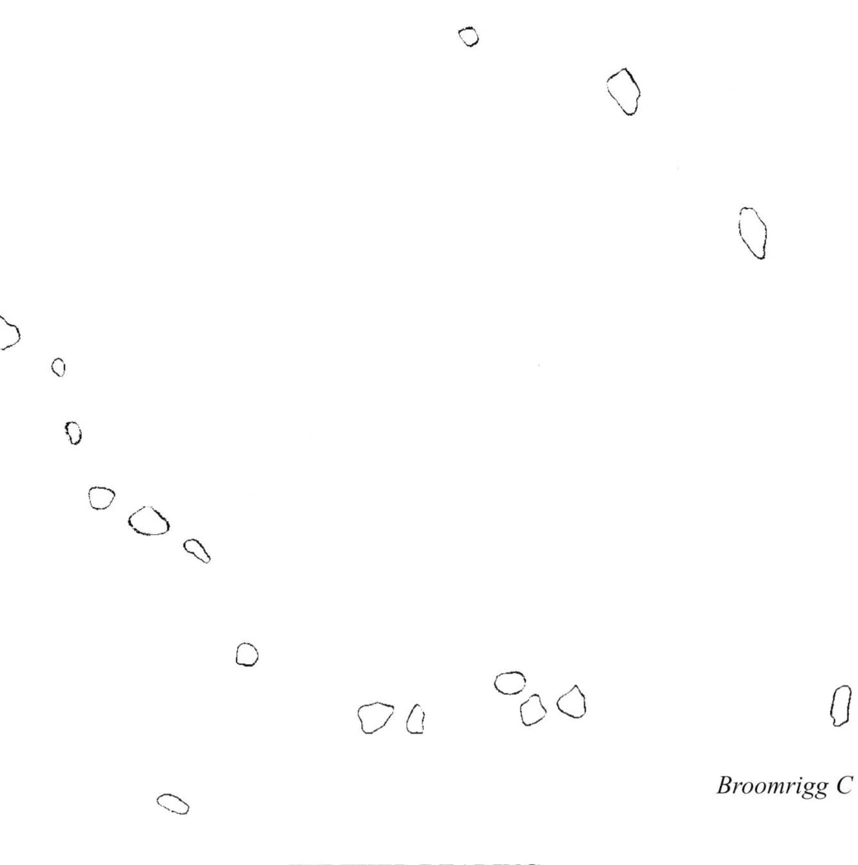

Broomrigg C

FURTHER READING:

Hodgson, K. S., *Notes on Stone Circles at Broomrigg, Grey Yauds, etc.*, TCWAAS, Volume 35, 1935.

Hodgson, K. S. and Harper, K., *The Prehistoric Site at Broomrigg near Ainstable: the Excavations of 1948-49*, TCWAAS, Volume 50, 1950.

Hodgson, K. S. 1952. *Further excavations at Broomrigg, near Ainstable.* TCWAAS. Volume 52.

Richardson, G. G. S. and Fell, C.I. 1975. *Unpublished excavations by the late Miss K.S. Hodgson.* TCWAAS. Volume 75.

7. THE BURNMOOR CIRCLES

White Moss NE.

GRID REF: Brat's Hill NY 1737 0233;
White Moss (SW) NY 1725 0239;
White Moss (NE) NY 1725 0239;
Low Longrigg (SW) NY 1725 0278;
Low Longrigg (NE) NY 1728 0281.

ELEVATION: Brat's Hill 260m (853ft);
White Moss (SW) 261m (856ft);
White Moss (NE) 260m (853ft);
Low Longrigg (SW) 279m (915ft);
Low Longrigg (NE) 280m (918ft).

MAP: OS Explorer (1:25000) OL6;
OS Landranger (1:50000) 96.

LOCATION: Brat's Hill Latitude N54.24.587;
Longitude WO 03.16.474:
White Moss (SW) Latitude N 54.24.614;
Longitude WO 03.16.584:
White Moss (NE) Latitude N 54.24.625;
Longitude WO 03.16.547:
Low Longrigg (SW) Latitude N 54.24.826;
Longitude WO 03.16.593:
Low Longrigg (NE) Latitude 54.24.841;
Longitude WO 03.16.567:
10km (6.2m) ENE of Ravenglass, 1.25km (0.8m) N of the village of Boot in Eskdale.

PARKING: Pay and display parking at Dalegarth Station – the terminus of the Ravenglass and Eskdale Railway.

WALKING DISTANCE:
Dalegarth Station to Brat's Hill – 2.23km (1.3m); White Moss – 2.42km (1.5m); Low Longrigg – 2.83km (1.7m).

TERRAIN: Steep bridleway, high exposed moorland, paths mainly good, but some faint or non-existent.

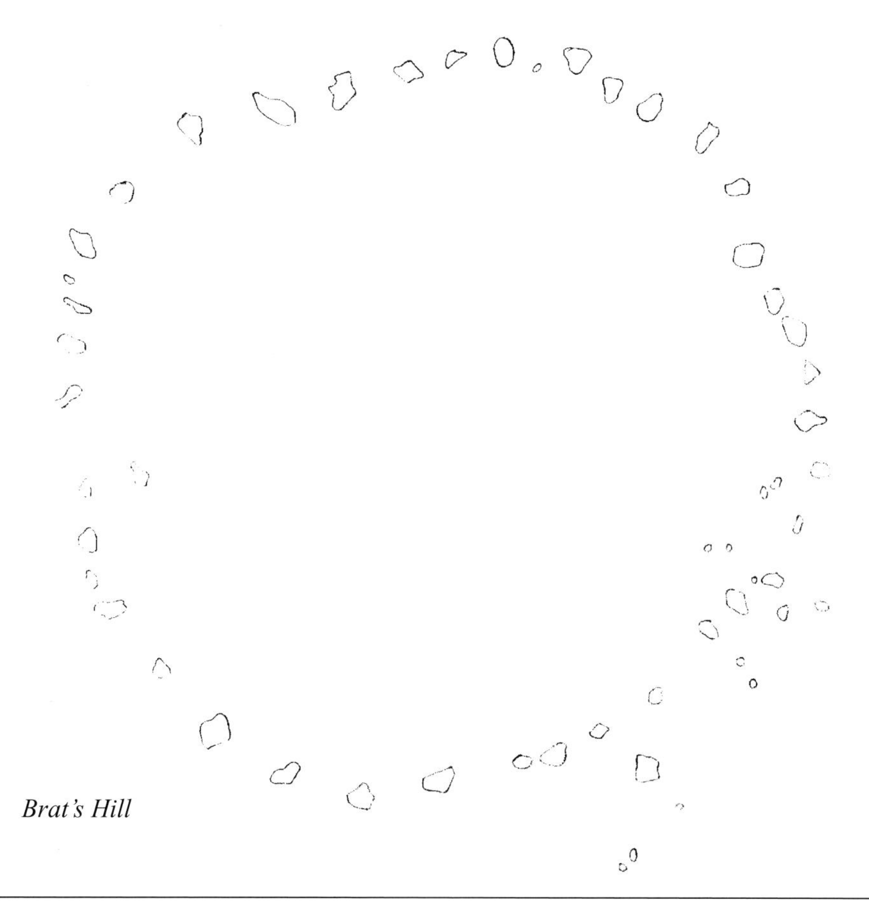

Brat's Hill

DETAILED DIRECTIONS:
In Boot follow the public bridleway for Burnmoor Tarn, Wasdale Head and Mitterdale across the bridge and past the Eskdale Corn Mill; the Brat's Hill stone circle is approximately 1.6km (1m) from here. After the gate turn right along the bridleway and commence the steep, strenuous climb to the moor. Continue N past a group of ruined cottages with the moor beginning to level out until the distinctive rocky outcrop of Acre Hows is reached. Brat's Hill stone circle is hidden behind the small hillock to the right of Acre Hows, and will shortly come into view SW of the bridleway. From Brat's Hill a path leads NW to the White Moss circles, which can be seen 100m (328ft) to the NW. The Low Longrigg circles are on the ridge forming the near horizon directly N from White Moss (NE). Leave White Moss (NE) by the NE path for 100m (340ft) then bear N uphill climbing, steadily to the top of the ridge and the Low Longrigg circles.

DESCRIPTION:

THE BURNMOOR circles have a magnificent setting upon this isolated high moor surrounded by dramatic mountain scenery, with the Scafell range to the NE and overlooking the valley of Mitterdale with views to the Irish Sea and the Isle of Man in the W. Burnmoor is thought to derive from 'borran', meaning a cairn of stones. Cairns are everywhere, but some may have resulted from field clearance during farming rather than being of a sepulchral nature.

Low Longrigg (SW) and Low Longrigg (NE)

Brat's Hill stone circle is the largest of the Burnmoor group. The circle is of irregular shape, consisting of approximately 42 stones, most of which are prostrate, with a diameter of about 32m (100ft) E-W and 26m (85ft) N-S, where the NNW arc of the circle is flattened. Seven of the stones are still standing, the tallest at the S being about 1m (3.2ft) in height. The inner area of the circle contains five cairns of 4 to 6m (13-20ft) in diameter. The tallest stone seems to align through the centre of the nearest cairn and the centre of the circle to the summit of Scafell to the NE. It has been claimed that some of the stones on the E and SE sides originate from Scafell, while the majority are of local granite from the moor.

Excavation in 1827 showed that each cairn had a dome of five stones and a kerb of fourteen stones, some of which contained fragments of burnt bone and antlers. It has been suggested that the cairn just S of the centre was the first to be constructed, and that the others were built around it. Brat's Hill shares a near-perfect conformity in size, shape and number of stones to Castlerigg stone circle some 24km (15m) to the N (see Castlerigg). An outlier to the NW is along a line joining the centres of Brat's Hill and White Moss (NE) and is thought to be orientated on the midsummer solstice sunset.

The two White Moss circles are on a NE-SW axis, sharing the same plateau of moorland as Brat's Hill, and are approximately 100m (328ft) distant. White Moss (NE) is perhaps the most impressive of all the Burnmoor circles. All eleven of its stones are still erect, varying in height from 0.5 to 1m (1.6 to 3.2ft) and forming a perfect circle with a diameter of 16m (52ft). About 45.7m (150ft) distant is White Moss (SW), which is of similar proportions, being a perfect circle with a diameter of 16.5m (54ft). It is more ruinous than its neighbour, with only a few of its fourteen stones still erect. Both circles contain a central

White Moss NE looking towards the Mitterdale estuary.

cairn. From these two circles the mountainous sides of the Mitterdale valley drop steeply in the W and seem to align on the distant mouth of the Mitterdale estuary and beyond to the Irish sea.

The two circles of Low Longrigg are some 385m (1260ft) N of the White Moss pair, and also share a NE-SW axis. Low Longrigg (NE) is the larger of the two circles. The circle consists of small stones in a ruinous state and of irregular shape, surrounding two cairns with a mean diameter of 21.5m (70ft). Low Longrigg (SW) is also ruinous, with small stones in a perfect circle with a diameter of 15m (49ft) surrounding a central cairn. The circles of Low Longrigg align on the saddle between Scafell summit and Horn Crag, where the sun rises at midsummer. From the high ridge of the Low Longrigg circles the aspect of Brat's Hill and the White Moss circles on the plain below can be better realised.

It has been suggested that this arrangement also reflects the order in which these monuments were constructed with Brat's Hill being the earliest circle, followed by White Moss and, shortly after, Low Longrigg, in the early Bronze Age. From the vantage point of the Low Longrigg circles there is an impression of similarity between the White Moss group and the Low Longrigg group. From Low Longrigg (NE), White Moss (NE) is directly S, both groups are roughly parallel and seem to mirror each other. The diameters and the distances between the centres of the cairns of both groups are also comparable.

FURTHER READING:

Clare, T, *Some Cumbrian Stone Circles in Perspective*, TCWAAS, Volume 75, 1975.

Dymond, C. W, *A Group of Cumberland Megaliths*, TCWAAS (O.S.), Volume V, 1881.

Williams, B, *On some Ancient Monuments in the County of Cumberland*, PSAL 3, 1856.

8. Casterton

Casterton from the east.

GRID REF:
SD 6393 7999.

ELEVATION:
160m (525 ft).

MAP:
OS Explorer (1:25 000) OL2;
OS Landranger (1:50000) 97.

LOCATION:
Latitude N 54.12.865;
Longitude WO 02.33.270;
3.5km (2.2m) NE of
Kirkby Lonsdale
and 1.5km (0.9m)
E of Casterton.

PARKING:
Restricted.

WALKING DISTANCE:
1km (0.6m).

TERRAIN:
Country lane, rutted track,
steep grassy hillside slope.

DESCRIPTION:
THE CIRCLE is located on a level terrace on a W facing slope of Casterton Fell, at the bottom of a steep hillside field which is littered with piles of stone. Its visibility from the track varies with the seasons. At times it is clearly discernible but in late summer it becomes almost invisible to the eye. To the E the fell ridge rises NNE to Casterton Fell, and to the W and S are extensive views across the vale of the Lune. Casterton is a well-defined embanked circle comprising of nineteen stones in an almost perfect circle with a diameter of 19m (62ft). The stones are not of a great height, although they are taller than other embanked circles. The tallest stones are to the S and SW, the tallest being approximately 50cm (20in), whereas many of the stones to the N are hardly visible.

Two stones marking the cardinal points E and W align with the centre of a saddle landform in the distant moors to the W above Kirkby Lonsdale. The saddle is created by the meeting of two moors of an almost identical appearance. Viewed from the immediate E of the circle this landform seems to be contained within the circle, with the saddle coinciding approximately with the centre. From here the lower ground level results in the circle being raised to eye level, and because of this the sun at the equinox can be seen to set simultaneously along this azimuth and into the centre of the circle.

The stones are set within an irregular bank of earth and stones, which provides

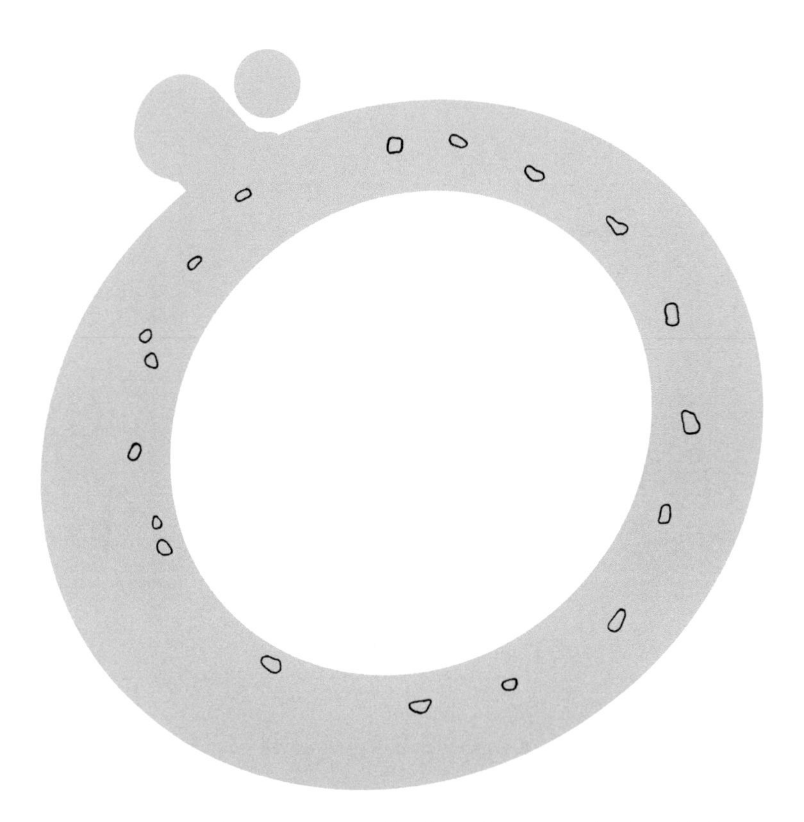

Casterton Stone Circle - plan drawn by Scruffy Crow.

DETAILED DIRECTIONS:
Just 0.5km (0.3m) S of Casterton on the A683 take the lane to the E for High Casterton. Continue for 0.5km (0.3m) to the next junction and take the lane opposite for Cowan Bridge and Settle. Cross the Roman road and take the lane for Bullpot, which a sign indicates is a no-through road. Continue along this lane past the public bridleway Bents Lane to the N, and continue uphill to the next public footpath on the left. Walk along the green lane towards Casterton Fell for 0.5km (0.3m). At the fifth field a gate to the W of the track gives access to the circle, which can be seen below, just within the far western wall of the field and S of a copse. On private land.

a levelled surface for the circle. The bank is highest from the E to the S and SW, where the land gradually slopes down towards the valley. To the W through to the N the bank is shallow and poorly defined, with the inner area of the circle almost level with the surrounding terrain. The inner face of the bank is not easily discernible but lies inside the stone circle.

Just outside the bank to the NNW is a feature which may be the remains of a cairn. No excavation of the site is known of, but a number of objects have been found in the vicinity of the circle. A report of a number of objects at a 'Druid's Temple' in 1828 is thought to have been at the Casterton stone circle. Among the finds were the head of a bronze spear, a flint arrowhead and possibly a beaker described as an 'antique drinking vessel'. The circle has been dated by an analysis of its archaeological traits to the early Bronze Age.

An alignment on a distant saddle landform.

9. CASTLERIGG

Castlerigg from the north.

DESCRIPTION:
THE MAIN approach to Castlerigg, from the car parking area towards the tall portal stones of the northern entrance, is the same today as it was for those who built the circle. Described as one of the most visually impressive stone circles in Britain, Castlerigg is an almost complete circle located on level ground on the top of Chestnut Hill, overlooking several valleys and set in a crown of mountains. It has been suggested that the location and geometry of Castlerigg were determined according to the surrounding mountains.

The portal of stones to the N frame the lowering fells of Lonscale and Blease, which mark the divide between the heights of Skiddaw to the W and Blencathra to the E, which dominate the skyline to the N. This aspect seems to be the main focus of the circle and it seems that Castlerigg was orientated towards this divide precisely between the summits of two of the most significant mountain ranges in Lakeland. This feature of orientation to the N was deemed so definite that it was used as the basis to determine the meridian and other bearings on the horizon in an early astronomical survey.

It must be stressed however that every survey of Castlerigg has located a different centre for the circle, although all within a few metres of each other. This demonstrates the difficulty of mapping an irregular circle of large stones which lack uniformity. The circle is also located in alignment between Helvellyn 10km (6m) SE and Skiddaw 6.5km (4m) NW. This alignment coincides with one of the proposed main axes of the circle's construction, a line which passes through stones J and C, and the centre of the circle aligns to the SE with the rising sun over Helvellyn at Candlemas/Samhain. In the opposite direction it marks the setting sun at the midsummer solstice over the western edge of Skiddaw.

There are solstice gatherings at midsummer to watch the sunset over Skiddaw, and then a vigil until dawn when the sun rises over Blencathra. Castlerigg is a principal location for observations of the Major Lunar Standstill – Thom proposed three azimuths for the moon, all significant to the major standstills. The most southerly moonrise indicated by one of Thom's constructional lines is from stone L to stone E, through the centre of the circle. The most southerly moonset and the most northerly moonset are also aligned from the centre of the circle through stones F and K; only the northerly moonrise is unaccounted for.

A simpler method of observing the southerly moonrise and moonset has been proposed using the large portal stones. Sighting across stone M to stone D marks the southerly moonrise, while the sightline across stone A to stone G marks the southerly moonset. The observation of the full moon's low arc across the sky at the southern standstill above Castlerigg, from moonrise to moonset, must be one of the most beautiful and stunning astronomical events. The Helvellyn mountain range, which forms the most extensive area of fells in the Lake District, is seen rising from the E towards the SSE.

Castlerigg is the most visited of all the Cumbrian circles. Thirty-eight of the original forty-two stones remain to form a flattened circle with diameters of 32.6m (107ft) and 29.9m (98ft). The stones are of local metamorphic slate and have a height ranging from 1-1.5m (3.2-4.9ft); the heaviest stone at the SE weighs approximately sixteen tons. There is also a stone some 75m (246ft) WSW of the circle at the edge of the field which has been described as an outlier and which has been suggested as marking sunrise for Beltane (1st May) and Lughnasa (1st August) looking ENE, and sunset at Imbolc (1st February) and Samhain (1st November) in the other direction. However this outlier is known to have been moved so there is some doubt over the accuracy of these alignments.

GRID REF:
NY 2914 2362.

ELEVATION:
212m (696ft).

MAP:
OS Explorer (1:25000) OL4;
OS Landranger (1:50000) 90.

LOCATION:
Latitude N 54.36.171;
Longitude WO 03.05.906:
2.5km (1.5m) E of Keswick.

PARKING:
Layby adjacent to site entrance.

WALKING DISTANCE:
110m (360ft) from car park.

TERRAIN:
Pasture.

The circle is thought to be one of the earliest, dating to the late Neolithic around 3200BC. It has been suggested that one of Castlerigg's main functions was connected with the stone axe industry in the Langdales, and three stone axes have been found within the circle, also consistent with an early date.

A report in 1856 stated that three cairns existed inside the circle, but whether they had been used for sepulchral purposes is not known. A faint circular feature visible in the grass in the NE sector of the circle may be the remains of one of these cairns. To the ESE is an internal rectangular setting of stones often described as the 'sanctuary', but which remains an unexplained feature. An excavation of this feature in 1882 found a pit 1m (3.2ft) deep to the W which contained earth, stones and charcoal. More recently a number of stone carvings have been found on the stones of the 'sanctuary', most notably a spiral on the inner face of stone B which has been photographed successfully even though nothing is visible to the eye. It is possible that this phenomenon is a result of the geological composition of the stone.

Among the many astronomical alignments claimed for the circle, stone B significantly features in marking both the equinox sunrise and sunset. Sighting over stone I to B indicates the equinox sunrise, while a line of sight over stone B to H marks the equinox sunset. Most remarkable of all is that the axis of the 'sanctuary' passes through stone B and aligns with Great Mell Fell which is 10.7km (6.6m) to the E. It has been suggested that this alignment also marks the horizon event of the rising star constellation of the

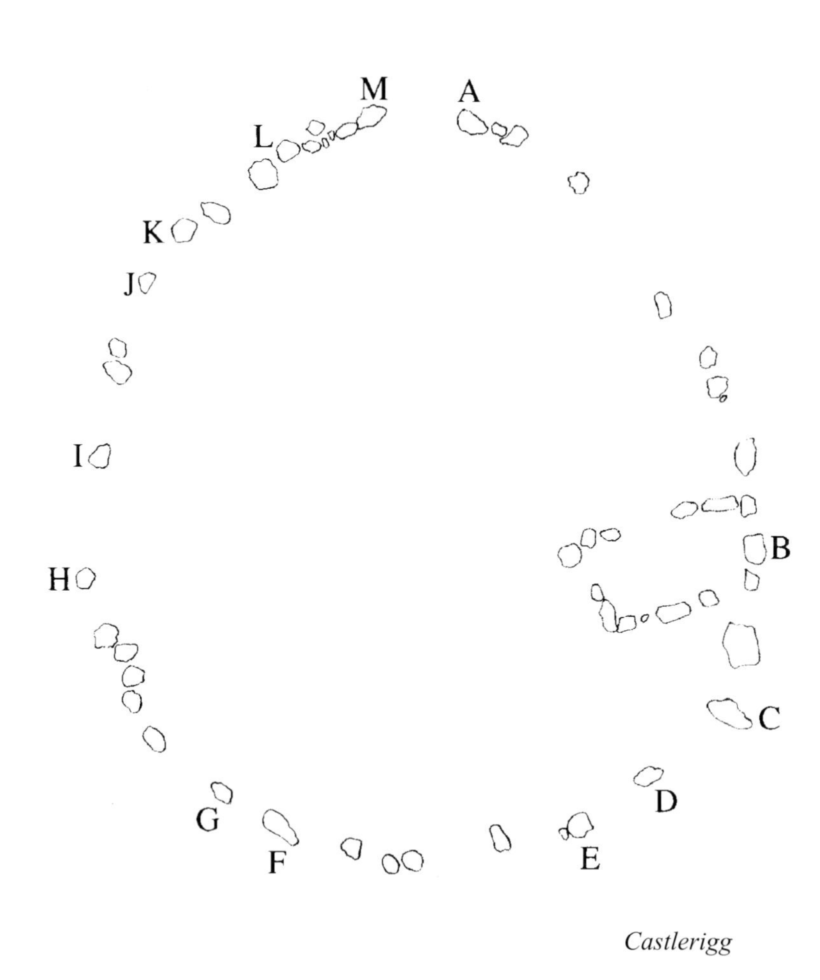

Castlerigg

DETAILED DIRECTIONS:
Castlerigg is signposted from the A66 E of Keswick. The site was bought by public subscription in 1913 and given to the National Trust, who manage the site for English Heritage.

Pleiades, heralding the approach of May and the beginning of summer. This alignment to Great Mell Fell was also the circumstance that occasioned the finding of a tumulus on Great Mell Fell, which was subsequently surveyed. The tumulus is at the centre of an earthwork described as 'a circular fosse, 6 or 7 inches deep and about 3 feet wide, the circle having a diameter of 60 feet, inside measurement'. Just S of true W it was noticed that the otherwise regular earthwork of the fosse had a feature which suggested an entrance to the central mound. This was approximately 1.2m (4ft) wide. It was found that 'a line drawn from the centre of the circular fosse through the middle of the gangway, if produced to the W, forms an alignment on the Castlerigg Circle'.

Castlerigg from the SW looking towards Blencathra.

FURTHER READING:

Anderson, W. D, *Some Recent Observations at the Keswick Stone Circle*, TCWAAS, Volume 15, 1915.
Anderson, W. D, *Plough-markings on Stones*, TCWAAS, Volume 23, 1923.
Clare, T, *Some Cumbrian Stone Circles in Perspective*, TCWAAS, Volume 75, 1975.
Dymond, C. W, *A Group of Cumberland Megaliths*, TCWAAS (O.S.), Volume 5, 1881.
Farrah, R W E, *Castlerigg – by the Light of the Silvery Moon*, Northern Earth, 105, 2006.
Farrah, R W E, *In Ancient Moonlight,* Northern Earth, 106, 2006.
Hood, S, *Cumbrian Stone Circles, the Calendar and the Issue of the Druids*, TCWAAS, Third Series, Volume 4, 2004.
Hood, S and Wilson, D, *Further Investigations into the Astronomical Alignments at Cumbrian Prehistoric Sites*, TCWAAS, Third Series, Volume 3, 2003.
Morrow, J, *Sun and Star Observations at the Stone Circles of Keswick and Long Meg*, Proceedings of the University of Durham Philosophical Society, 1909.
Williams, B, *On some Ancient Monuments in the County of Cumberland*, PSAL 3, 1856.

10. Elva Plain

Elva Plain from the W looking towards Skiddaw.

GRID REF:
NY 1770 3171.

ELEVATION:
224m (735ft).

MAP:
OS Explorer (1:25000) OL4;
OS Landranger (1:50000) 90.

LOCATION:
Latitude N 54.40.426;
Longtitude WO 03.16.663:
5.5km (3.4m) E of Cockermouth near Elva Plain Farm, W of the northern end of Bassenthwaite Lake.

PARKING:
Restricted.

WALKING DISTANCE:
0.4km (0.2m).

TERRAIN:
Fellside pasture.

DESCRIPTION:
THE CIRCLE is sited on the level terrace of Elva Plain, on a S-facing slope of Elva Hill above the valley of the River Derwent. The high plateau looks eastward across Bassenthwaite Lake to Skiddaw and the Caldbeck fells; to the S are the lower slopes of the Lorton fells. Skiddaw is the main focus of the site, with Elva Plain framing the mountain and its levelled summit central to the circle. From this direction Skiddaw has a pleasing cone-like symmetry. From the centre of the ring the equinoctial sun will be seen to rise above the heights of the mountain.

There are fifteen surviving stones from a possible thirty, in a large, almost perfect circle with a diameter of approximately 34m (110ft). The stones, all of volcanic ash, have now fallen and are not very impressive; some lie level with the ground. The largest stone is to the W, with a height of 0.7m (2.2ft). The circle was surveyed early in the twentieth century recording the existence of an outlier some 55.4m (182ft) from the centre of the circle to the SW, but there is no longer any visible trace of this. Outliers to stone circles often suggest directional trends, and the outlier to the Elva Plain circle in the SW, positioned along the narrow ridge towards the coast, suggests such a tendency.

The circle has been classified as one of the great open circles and probably dates from the mid to late Neolithic. The name Elva has its origins in Elfhow, by which it was known in 1488, possibly deriving from the Old Norse name for Elva Hill, elfhaugr meaning 'the hill of the malignant elves'. One possible explanation of this is the association of the circle with the distribution of stone axes from the central fells. One of the principal suggested routes leading from the central fells heads NW towards the coastal plain, passing close to the Elva Plain stone circle. Although there are no records of stone axes being found at Elva Plain, such prehistoric axes were often referred to as 'elf shot'.

Elva Plain

FURTHER READING:

Anderson, W D, *Elva Stone Circle*, TCWAAS, Volume 23, 1923.
Hodgson, K S, *Proceedings 301*, TCWAAS, Volume 63, 1963.

DETAILED DIRECTIONS:
Turn off the A66 following the B5291 alongside Bassenthwaite Lake to Castle Inn. At the bridge continue straight ahead following sign 'Higham Hall – 1 mile'. Continue past Higham Hall for a distance of 0.6km (0.4m), where a gate to the N of the road, shortly before Elva Plain Farm, leads to a Public Access Route through an environmentally sensitive area. Head NW uphill towards a gate on the brow of a rise: the stone circle can be seen to the NW. The path to the circle is signposted.

11. GAMELANDS

Gamelands from the W.

GRID REF:
NY 6400 0816.

ELEVATION:
265m (869ft).

MAP:
OS Explorer (1:25000) OL19;
OS Landranger (1:50000) 91.

LOCATION:
Latitude N 54.28.057;
Longitude WO 02.33.415:
4.3km (2.6m) NE of Tebay,
1.6km (0.9m) E of Orton.

PARKING:
Restricted.

WALKING DISTANCE:
Negligible.

TERRAIN:
Fellside pasture.

DESCRIPTION:

THERE ARE traces of an embankment visible around the Gamelands stone circle, although the low bank is now very difficult to discern. All the stones have now fallen and none now attain a height of more than 1m (3.2ft), which makes the circle elusive, being well hidden behind the dry stone walling. There are approximately forty surviving stones, all of Shap granite, except for one due S of the centre which is limestone. Some of the smaller stones may be the remnants of larger ones, for it is recorded that some of the stones were subjected to blasting and others buried to make the ground easier to plough. The land was first ploughed in 1863, and the plough was taken right through the circle.

Gamelands has been classified as one of the great open circles and probably dates from the mid to late Neolithic. It is a flattened circle and one of the largest in Cumbria, with diameters measuring 44.4m (145ft) from E to W and 38.8m (127ft) N to S. There is a possible entrance in the SE section of the circle. The stones in the southern arc are located on higher land than the rest, and beyond the entrance the land falls away towards the SE.

A recent topographical survey has shown the circle seems to enclose the head of a valley which slopes downwards in a similar fashion to Long Meg, with the possibility that the circle also enclosed a spring.

A sandstone slab, possibly unearthed during ploughing in the central area, lay near the perimeter of the circle due W of the centre. It is thought that this may have been a cist cover although no interments have ever been found and the slab has since disappeared. The circle lies directly below Knott Hill to the N, which dominates the local skyline and is the highest point on Great Asby Scar.

Gamelands

FURTHER READING:

Fell, C I, *Proceedings 408*, TCWAAS, Volume 64, 1964.

Ferguson, R S, *Stone Circle at Gamelands, Bland House Brow, Township of Raisbeck, Parish of Orton, Westmorland*, TCWAAS, Volume 6, 1883.

DETAILED DIRECTIONS:

On the B6260 Appleby to Tebay road. Just W of Orton village centre take the road signed Gaisgill – Raisbeck – Kirkby Stephen. After Scarside take the next left up the public bridleway Knott Lane, opposite a plantation. Access is through the second gate to the E, approximately 129.5m (425ft) distant. Turn left into the field and head for the gate immediately ahead with the surviving gable end of a barn beyond. The stone circle will come into view. Private land - access permission required.

12. GLASSONBY

Glassonby from the S.

GRID REF:
NY 5727 3934.

ELEVATION:
130m (427ft).

MAP:
OS Explorer (1:25000) OL5;
OS Landranger (1:50000) 91.

LOCATION:
Latitude N 54.44.837;
Longitude WO 02.39.912:
1km (0.6m) NW of Glassonby village, 10.4km (6.5 miles) NNE of Penrith.

PARKING:
Restricted.

WALKING DISTANCE:
Negligible.

TERRAIN:
Fellside pasture.

DESCRIPTION:
THE GLASSONBY circle is defined as a cairn-circle and its finest aspect is from the gate to the S. The stones have an average height of 0.6m (2ft), and were once covered by a mound of water-worn cobbles. The tumulus was estimated to be approximately 30.4m (100ft) in diameter, approximately twice the size of the circle. The northern Lakeland fells can be seen across the Eden valley to the W and the Pennines dominate the skyline to the E, with Cross Fell the highest point of the Pennine chain to the ESE.

The stones of the circle were not sunk into the earth but placed at ground level and supported by the cobbles which formed the mound. The circle is partly ruined but once consisted of some thirty stones of different types. It has an oval form, with approximate diameters of 15.6m (51ft) by 14m (46ft). The stones were set close together, forming a continuous wall.

The circle had several carved stones but only one survives in situ; this is the southern-most stone of a row of six to the E. The stone is lightly carved with concentric circles, ovoids and chevrons. The carvings are so faint that they are very difficult to discern and went unnoticed at the time of the excavation report in 1900. A missing stone once existed either in the SSE or SSW, which was reported as being of sandstone, measuring over 0.9m (3ft) long, 0.1m (0.5ft) in width and 0.6m (2ft) high incised with a spiral or concentric circles on its side 'like the figure on Long Meg'.

There are several gaps in the circle but an opening to S is more prominent and may have been the position of this once remarkable Long Meg-like stone. From the centre of the circle a distinctive saddle feature on the far Pennine horizon is directly N. A burial cist, which can still be seen, was found beneath the mound just inside the circle in the SSE,

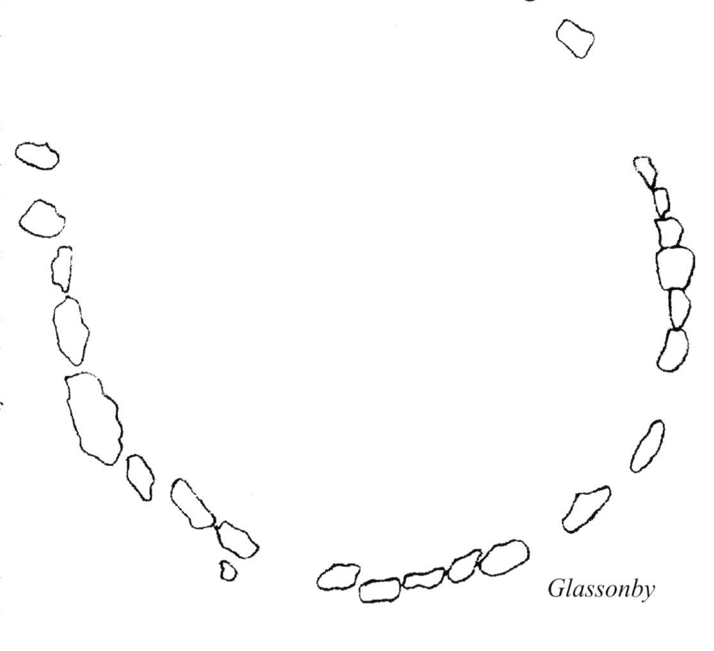
Glassonby

FURTHER READING:
Collingwood, W.G, *Tumulus at Grayson-lands, Glassonby, Cumberland,* TCWAAS, Volume 1, 1901.
Thornley, W, *Ring-marked Stones at Glassonby and Maughanby*, TCWAAS, Volume 2, 1902.

DETAILED DIRECTIONS:
Not signposted. Turn right near a 'Reduce Speed Now' road sign, along a tarmac lane 0.3km (0.2m) N of the village before the road descends to Daleraven bridge. Access is through a gate a few metres to the left of the driveway. From the gate the circle can be seen to the NNW in the corner of the lower pasture. Private land - access permission required.

although nothing was found inside. Two cremations were found outside the circle, one in a collared urn in the SE approximately 3m (10ft) from the circumference of the circle in the vicinity of the surviving carved stone. The other interment was a deposit of bone in a hole made in the surface of the ground.

The only other notable find was a bead of light blue faience with a wavy line of opaque white, which was found near the surface inside the circle in the NNW. The urn and bead are dated to the early Bronze Age and both are now in Tullie House Museum, Carlisle. The presence of a ring ditch in the same field has been reported recently; it is said to be the terminal of a cursus.

On the opposite bank of the Daleraven valley to the NNE is the farm of Old Parks approximately 0.75km (0.4m) distant. In 1892 Cumberland County Council purchased a pile of stone, thought to be field clearance for roadworks. It was soon evident that the heap of stone was an ancient burial mound, and several interments were found. At the centre of the mound were five large monoliths in a line exactly N to S. The slabs measure 0.51-0.96m (1.6-3.1ft) in length, 0.16-0.33m (0.5-1.1ft) in width and have an approximate height of 0.61m (2ft). Three of the five stones had carvings of similar characteristics, depicting a series of spirals, concentric arcs, crooks, circular enclosures and angular enclosures. Two of these, the most southerly stones, survive and can be seen in Tullie House. The partly-dismantled mound was photographed showing the stones in situ before the cairn was completely destroyed.

Glassonby from the S.

13. The Gretigate Circles

The remains of Gretigate B.

DETAILED DIRECTIONS:

Take the track (marked by 'Public Footpath') to the W of the A595, just N of the B5344. This is the Gretigate or 'gravel road' which leads to Seascale Hall. After approximately 0.5km (0.3m), take the turning on the right just before a bungalow. This track broadens into a cul-de-sac clearing which has been used as a tip for spoil. A double wooden gate to the right of the cul-de-sac leads onto farmland. Turn left along the edge of the field for about 33m (110ft) to Gretigate A. Back at the cul-de-sac a track to the left of the plantation leads into the enclosure of wood and thicket. The path continues ahead through the plantation which leads to an area of sedge grass and, eventually, leads to Gretigate B and C just before a pond. Private Land - access permission required.

DESCRIPTION:

THERE IS very little in the way of reward for even the enthusiast visiting the Gretigate circles, for they are ruinous. They are included here because the site was once of some importance. Its near-miraculous discovery late in the 1950s was due to an observant eye able to discern amongst the confusion of 'many stones... the outlines of what... was a stone circle'. This was Gretigate A, the largest of the group and what must have once been a magnificently-located circle.

The reason for its destruction was cultivation, for it would have been an impediment to the plough. The sense of loss is tangible and deepens our appreciation for all the other stone circles which have disappeared, together with their landscapes. The ruinous state of the circles B & C is very likely the result of drilling exploration by the nuclear fuels industry while looking for a suitable area for underground storage. My informant, a local farmer recalls, that this work took place after the discovery and excavation of the circles in the late 1950s, when the site was already in a derelict state.

The exploratory work has further added to the confusion of the remains, but three stone circles have been identified. The largest circle (A) to the E was identified by a change in the appearance of an earth and cobble hedge to the NE of the enclosure, running NW-SE. The hedge is generally straight but changes into the arc of a stone wall some 27.4m (90ft) in length, which curves into the enclosure before rejoining the hedge. Within this stone arc were noticed several large stones, and on the inside of the arc was a collection of large stones which had been removed during ploughing and

Pictured above, one of the stones from the Gretigate C stone circle.

GRID REF:
Gretigate A - NY 0578 0369;
Gretigate B & C - NY 0571 0370.

ELEVATION:
80m (262ft).

MAP:
OS Explorer (1:25000) OL6;
OS Landranger (1:50000) 89.

LOCATION:
Gretigate A -
Latitude N 54.25.189;
Longitude WO 03.27.215:
Gretigate B & C -
Latitude N 54.25.203;
Longitude WO 03.27.280:
1km (0.5miles) W of Gosforth.

PARKING:
Restricted at the cul-de-sac at the end of the track clearing.

WALKING DISTANCE:
Negligible.

TERRAIN:
Agricultural, plantation, sedge grass and mire.

had 'obviously formed part of the circle at one time'. Two of the largest boulders, which are uniform in size, seem to be, amazingly, undisturbed. These are found at the apex of what was the SW arc of the circle. It was concluded that this was once the arc of a large stone circle approximately 31.6m (104ft) in diameter. The land rises to the NE, but there is a magnificent panorama of Lakeland fells from the ENE to the SSE, with Scafell due E from what was once the centre of the circle.

The two circles to the W (B & C) are within the enclosure just before the pond, and are located within a shallow valley. The circle B to the S is the largest with an irregular diameter of between 18.8-21.9m (62-72ft). This adjoins the smaller circle C to the N which has a diameter of approximately 7.3m (24ft). These latter circles were partially excavated. It is thought that the larger circle B consisted of about fifteen to sixteen stones, of which nine remained at the time of excavation. Circle C originally consisted of twelve stones, nine of which remain. Both circles B & C contained central cairns which would date them to the Bronze Age. Very little was found in circle B other than three areas of burnt earth, two holes containing carbonised wood and a worn tooth. In Circle C two small flints were found near one of the stones, and near the central area were some small carbon deposits, a small egg-sized granite ball and possibly some burnt bone fragments.

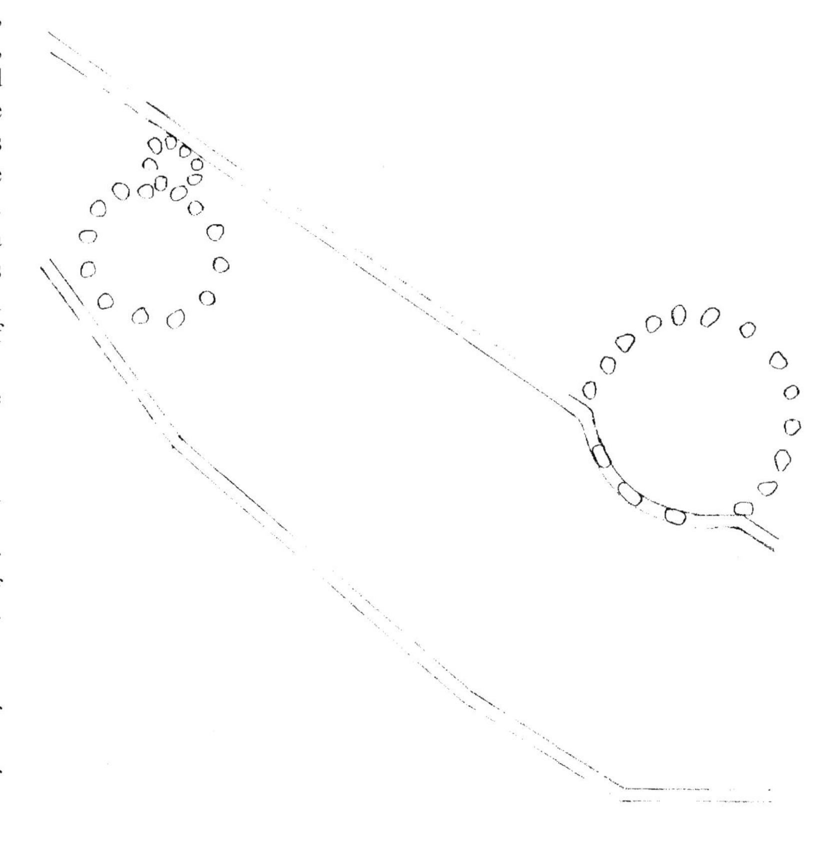

The Gretigate Stone Circles

FURTHER READING:

Stout, H B, *Gretigate Stone Circles, Sides, Gosforth*, TCWAAS, Volume 61, 1961.

14. Grey Croft

Grey Croft from the SW.

GRID REF:
NY 0333 0238.

ELEVATION:
25m (82ft).

MAP:
OS Explorer (1:25000) OL6;
OS Landranger (1:50000) 89.

LOCATION:
Latitude; 54.24.459;
Longitude; 03.29.450:
3.5km (2.25miles)
WSW of Gosforth,
near Seascale Hall Farm.

PARKING:
Restricted.

WALKING DISTANCE:
0.9km (0.6m).

TERRAIN:
Lowland pasture.

DESCRIPTION:

GREY CROFT has a surreal setting, with the cooling towers of Sellafield nuclear power station just 1km (0.6m) to the N, but in total contrast the shoreline is just 0.5km (0.3m) to the W, affording open views of the Irish Sea and the Isle of Man. The circle is sited on a low crest within a rich pasture of approximately 31 acres, known as Grey Crofts. It is located 320m (350yds) NW of Seascale Farm, with the highest Lakeland fells to the E.

All but one of the twelve stones of the circle was destroyed in 1820 by a tenant farmer, who buried them without permission of the landowner because their presence made ploughing impractical. The restoration of the circle took place in 1948 and is thought to have been accurate and 'highly successful'. The stones were toppled over into pits which had been dug for them, and buried to a depth varying from 0.9-1.5m (3-5ft). Often, the original packing stones which helped support the stones were left in situ. Many of the stones were found in an inclined position which helped determine which was the base end. Traces of weathering from the prevailing

Grey Croft

DETAILED DIRECTIONS:

Turn off the A595 taking the B5344 for Seascale. Turn right towards BNFL Calder Gate; the footpath is signposted either side of the road 0.9km (0.6m) from the junction near Seascale Hall Farm. The Public Footpath to the W marks a stile located below the roadside barrier, and the stone circle can be seen from here to the WSW. Cross the stile and follow the farm track round to a ruined farmhouse, taking another stile to the NE. After 0.3km (0.2m) another stile allows access to a field with a direct permissive path to the stone circle. However, this can sometimes necessitate walking across a cultivated field; to avoid this, take the short detour following the field fence SW to the gate ahead, which gives access to pasture. Follow the field fence uphill in an easterly direction and the stone circle soon comes into view. The path from the ruined farmhouse is a Defra conservation walk through an environmentally sensitive area which is being managed to benefit wading birds (such as curlew), as well as grey partridge and tree sparrow.

Grey Croft from the E.

winds also helped during restoration.

There are ten of the original twelve stones remaining, set in a flattened circle with diameters of 27m by 24m (88.5ft by 78.7ft). It has been suggested that the builders exercised some care in the selection of stones, as with one exception all the stones are of local Borrowdale volcanic lava and of fairly regular height, between 1.5-2m (4.9-6.5ft). There was a small outlier at some distance to the N but this is no longer in position. It is thought to have been removed in recent years and placed within the circle.

The stones surround the dome of a central burial cairn which is oval in shape, measuring 6.7 by 4.5m (22ft by 15ft). The stones of the cairn were mainly red sandstone. The stones at the centre of the cairn are smaller than those defining its perimeter. Traces of fire, charcoal and burnt bones were found within the cairn. A fragment of a jet or lignite ring was found under the eastern edge of the cairn, helping date the cairn to the early Bronze Age. A broken Neolithic stone axe was found buried at the base of a stone to the E, and other stone axes have been found in the vicinity, suggesting an earlier, Neolithic date for the circle. It seems likely that the circle lies at the coastal end of a trade route for axes from the central fells through Eskdale.

FURTHER READING:

Fletcher, W, *Grey Croft Stone Circle, Seascale, Cumberland*, TCWAAS, Volume 57, 1957.

15. GUNNERKELD

GRID REF:
NY 5682 1774.

ELEVATION:
265m (869ft).

MAP:
OS Explorer (1:25000) OL5;
OS Landranger (1:50000) 90.

LOCATION:
Latitude N 54.33.188;
Longitude WO 02.40.140:
2.5km (1.5 miles) NNE of Shap.

PARKING:
Restricted.

WALKING DISTANCE:
0.5km (0.3m).

TERRAIN:
Confused, pathless moorland, extensive marsh.

DESCRIPTION:
IT APPEARS that this circle takes the name of Gunnerkeld, meaning 'Sportsman's Spring' from the nearby Sike. There is a surreal contrast between the turbulent noise of the motorway traffic just metres away and the broken peace of this ancient circle. The circle is sited on a low-level limestone terrace within a valley, which slopes towards the NNW, and a depression of marsh. Gunnerkeld is two concentric circles, possibly combining aspects of an earlier outer stone circle with an early Bronze Age inner cairn circle. The outer circle has a diameter of approximately 31.8m (104ft) N to S and 29m (95ft) E to W with an inner ring diameter of 15.5m (51ft) N to S and 14.5m (47ft) E to W.

Gunnerkeld

A survey in the 1870s found that most of the stones of the outer circle had fallen, although two of the largest to the N were still standing. All but one of the estimated thirty stones of the inner circle are prostrate. The stones of the outer circle are generally larger than those of the inner ring and consist of Carboniferous limestone and Shap granite. The two large stones to the N of the outer circle are reminiscent of the northern portal stones at Castlerigg, and the dimensions of the two circles are almost identical (see Castlerigg). It has been suggested that both may have been built by the same megalithic architect. If the outer circle of Gunnerkeld is of the same age as Castlerigg, then the inner ring was a later addition, dating to the late Neolithic period. Supporting this is the fact that the mound does not coincide with the N-S axis of the circle which passes through the northern portal stones.

The low mound in the central area of the inner circle is a burial cairn with the remains of a cist still visible. A depression in the centre was made prior to the survey of the 1870s, and is probably linked to the destruction of the cist and its contents.

FURTHER READING:
Dymond, C W, *Gunnerkeld Stone Circle*, TCWAAS, Volume 4, 1880.

DETAILED DIRECTIONS:
Two kilometres (1.25m) N of Shap on the A6 take the minor road to the E for Sleagill. Shortly after crossing over and under M6 take the minor road for Little Strickland, and then take the track to Gunnerwell Farm. Gunnerkeld is W of the farm. Take the track in front of the farmhouse, through the gate on the right, bearing SW downhill through the trees, heading for the dry stone wall. Access can be difficult in wet weather, with Gunnerkeld Sike between the farm and stone circle. Private land.

Gunnerkeld Stone Circle from the E.

16. Hird Wood

Hird Wood from the E.

DESCRIPTION:
THE CIRCLE is located on a small shoulder of land on the steep side of the valley. It looks across to the low fell of the Tongue to the NE and the higher fells of Ill Bell and Yoke beyond. The course of the ancient way known for the Roman road High Street runs below these fells into Trout Beck valley. There is very little of the circle surviving, possibly due to the path which passes through it. The circle undoubtedly came first, but because it was sited on the only shoulder of land on the side of a steep valley, what was an ancient way evolved and with time preference was given to the highway.

The circle was further marginalized during enclosure, its stones becoming the foundation stones of the wall. The tallest stone is about 1m (3.3ft) in height and is located on the NW edge of a what appears to be a central mound. This stone has a clearly defined N-S axis which, incidentally, follows the line of the path. There are three surviving standing stones,

GRID REF:
NY 4162 0591.

ELEVATION:
236m (774ft).

MAP:
OS Explorer (1:25000) OL7;
OS Landranger (1:50000) 90.

LOCATION:
Latitude N 54.26.719;
Longitude WO 02.54.099:
4km (2.4m) NE of Ambleside.

PARKING:
A small lay-by to the W of the A592, N of Troutbeck and adjacent to Town Head.

WALKING DISTANCE:
2.1km (1.3m).

TERRAIN:
Narrow bridleway through steep woodland – grass and stone track.

which are incorporated in the base of the ruined dry stone wall to the W.

From the S some semblance of the original circle is evident in the curvature of these stones and the wall. The line of the circle's continuation can be traced in a group of three stones in the northern arc, now prone and partly buried.

The circle has been described as two concentric circles and possibly once had a similar aspect to Gunnerkeld (see Gunnerkeld), on a much smaller scale, with a large circle of approximately 19.8m (65ft) surrounding what appears to be an inner cairn circle, although some doubt surrounds its authenticity. The presence of a roughed-out stone axe found nearby, associated with the circle may indicate a late Neolithic date (similar to Gunnerkeld), whereas the cairn, if it is a burial mound, would suggest a later early Bronze Age date.

FURTHER READING:

Cowper, H S, *Unrecorded and Unusual Types of Stone Implements*, TCWAAS, Volume 34, 1934.

Hird Wood

DETAILED DIRECTIONS:
Approximately 250m (820ft) N of the lay-by, shortly after a small ravine, take the grassy track to the E of the road marked 'Public Bridleway'. This track leads eventually to Hird Wood stone circle, approximately 1.3km (0.9m) distant. The path keeps to a contour halfway up the W side overlooking the peaceful Troutbeck valley. Continue along the bridleway through a couple of gateways; with Trout Beck making a loop in the valley below, the path begins to rise steeply through a small wood passing the whitewashed walls of Troutbeck Park Farm far below. A small gateway leads into an area of pasture where a section of ruined dry stone wall to the west of the track can be seen ahead; this marks the approximate site of the stone circle.

17. The Iron Hill Stone Circles

White Hag from the N.

GRID REF:
Castlehowe Scar NY 5875 1547;
Iron Hill (N) NY 5963 1483; Iron Hill (S) NY 5964 1476;
Oddendale NY 5920 1290; White Hag NY 6072 1159.

ELEVATION:
Castlehowe Scar 315m (1033ft); Iron Hill (N) 350m (1148ft);
Iron Hill (S) 350m (1148ft); Oddendale 335m (1099ft);
White Hag 330m (1082ft).

MAP:
OS Explorer (1:25000) OL5 & OL19;
OS Landranger (1:50000) 91.

LOCATION:
Castlehowe Scar - Latitude N 54.31.970;
Longitude W 02.38.338:
Iron Hill (N) - Latitude 54.31.625;
Longitude WO 02.37.512:
Iron Hill (S) - Latitude N 54.31.593;
Longitude WO 02.37.506:
Oddendale - Latitude N 54.30.591;
Longitude WO 02.37.899:
White Hag - Latitude N 54.29.891;
Longitude WO 02.36.476:
6.5km (4 miles) W of Crosby Ravensworth
or 2.8km (1.7m) E of Shap.

PARKING:
On roadside grass verges for all sites except White Hag.

WALKING DISTANCE:
Castlehowe Scar – negligible; Iron Hill (N) & Iron Hill (S) –
0.7km (0.4m); Oddendale – 0.7km (0.4m);
White Hag – 2.8km (1.7m).

TERRAIN:
Country lane, bridlepath, grassy fell, rugged moorland

Iron Hill North and South

DETAILED DIRECTIONS:
At Crosby Ravensworth Village Hall follow road W to Shap, continue past a plantation and turn left at road sign for Oddendale; alternatively, from Shap, turn off the A6 for Crosby Ravensworth. At the turn for Oddendale, Castlehowe Scar stone circle is on the right in a small field. Continue along the road to Oddendale, bearing left beside the Hardendale Quarry; the Iron Hill comes into view with the circles Iron Hill North and Iron Hill South on the skyline. The circles are a short walk uphill along the Haberwain Lane public footpath. Continue S and park in the vicinity of Oddendale Farm. Follow the public bridleway S for Crosby Ravenworth – Sproat Ghyll, past an area of limestone pavement on the right and head SSW onto the moor towards two massive Shap granite boulders. Oddendale stone circle is approximately 120m (400ft) ahead. For the White Hag stone circle, continue S along the public bridleway past a plantation and small wood, bear left along the permissive path towards the corner of a plantation and climb uphill towards a cairn on the skyline, to the right of two isolated trees. At the hollowed-out cairn identified by a wooden post, take the path heading in an ESE direction, towards a small enclosure built with limestone pavement directly ahead. Continue along this cairn-enclosure alignment for approximately 200m (650ft) to the low-lying stones of White Hag. Alternatively, for the more energetic, all five of these stone circles can be visited within a 17km (10m) circular walk from Crosby Ravensworth. Castlehowe Scar is on private land.

Iron Hill North from the S.

DESCRIPTION:

THE IRON HILL stone circles are on a high limestone plateau, between Crosby Ravensworth and Shap, which has a wealth of Neolithic and early Bronze Age monuments. With the exception of Castlehowe Scar, the group are regarded as skyline barrows – barrows located on summits and clearly visible on the skyline from the valleys they overlook. Because of their greater prominence in the landscape, and being nearer the heavens, it has been suggested that compared with the barrows found lower down, skyline barrows belong to a group of particular significance.

They lie on a N-S axis, and can all be accessed from the track which runs from Castlehowe Scar in the N to White Hag in the S. These moors must have been of great significance, possessing as they do such a profusion of ancient cairns and circles. The circles of Castlehowe Scar, Iron Hill North and South and Oddendale all possess marked cardinal trends. All five circles consist almost entirely of the distinctive pink Shap granite.

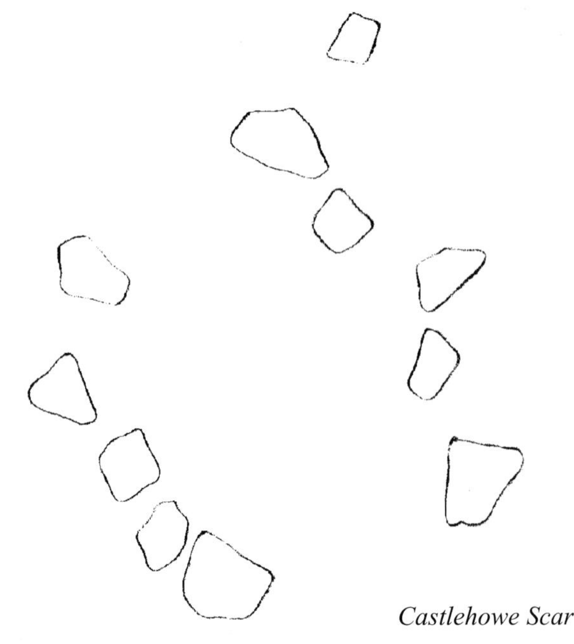

Castlehowe Scar

The small circle of Castlehowe Scar is sited in a field beside a stone wall and consists of ten stones with a diameter of approximately 7m (23ft); the tallest stone stands to a height of 1m (3.3ft). Castlehowe Scar has the appearance of a cairn circle but no trace of a mound survives. From the circle the small saddle form of Coalpit Hill, approximately 4.5km (2.8m) distant, marks the highest point on the horizon, where a large tumulus measuring 18.5m (60.6ft) in diameter and approximately 2.2m (7.2ft) in height, is sited to the NE of the triangulation pillar.

The circles of Iron Hill are in close proximity and aligned N to S. Both are clearly visible on the skyline from below being sited on top of the hill. The one to the N is a cairn circle which is perfectly bisected by a dry stone wall. The low boulders surrounding the cairn are clearly visible on the southern side, the tallest being about 75cm (2.4ft). The cairn is on the highest point of the hill and commands extensive views to the eastern

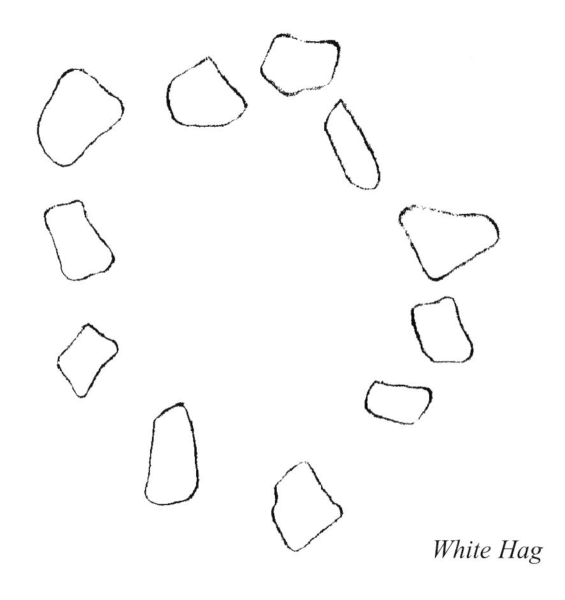

White Hag

Oddendale from the E.

Lakeland fells in the W, the Howgill fells in the S and the pastoral valleys of the Lyvennet and the Eden in the E, with the Pennines beyond.

The southern circle, about 60m (200ft) downhill, has a set of stones which form a ring around the hollowed centre of a low mound. The stones are larger than the northern circle, the tallest being just over 1m (3.3ft). Excavation in the 1860s revealed the bones of 'a man of great stature, a portion of the antler of a deer, much larger than those of our days, and bones of other animals'.

Oddendale is the most impressive of the Iron Hill circles. Sited on the brow of a low hill, the circle consists of two almost perfect concentric circles. The outer circle has thirty four stones and a diameter of approximately 27m (90ft), whereas the inner is an almost continuous kerb of stones around a low mound, with a diameter of 7.5m (25ft). The stones of both circles are low, though the stones of the outer circle are larger than the inner circle. From the centre of the circle directly S, the saddle of Coalpit Hill marks the high point of the near horizon now 2km (1.2m) distant, and directly W is another prominent saddle landform in the distant Lakeland fells and to the SE is the mound of Seal Howe.

Just outside the main circle to the N is a feature which has been interpreted as a smaller circle or cairn approximately 4.3m (14ft) in diameter. Most of the stones of this satellite circle are either totally or partially buried, but one large stone lies prone directly N of the centre of Oddendale. From this stone a line of sight passes through the centre of the two Oddendale circles and aligns on Coalpot Hill. The great circle of Oddendale overlooks the largest settlement on these moors, Ewe Close, approximately 1.6km (1m) distant to the E. A Bronze Age settlement, it was deemed important enough for the Romans to route the Lancaster to Carlisle road within 18m (60ft) of the settlement.

At the southern limit of this group of circles are the eleven fallen stones of White Hag. This circle shares some similarity with Castlehowe Scar in size, with a diameter of 6m (20ft). Its stones, however are more inconspicuous, and smaller. White Hag, like the other skyline barrows of the Iron Hill group, is blessed with wonderful panoramas overlooking the Lyvennet valley and many of these cairns can be seen on the distant skyline. Some 10m (32.8ft) ENE are a group of boulers which possibly belong to another small circle.

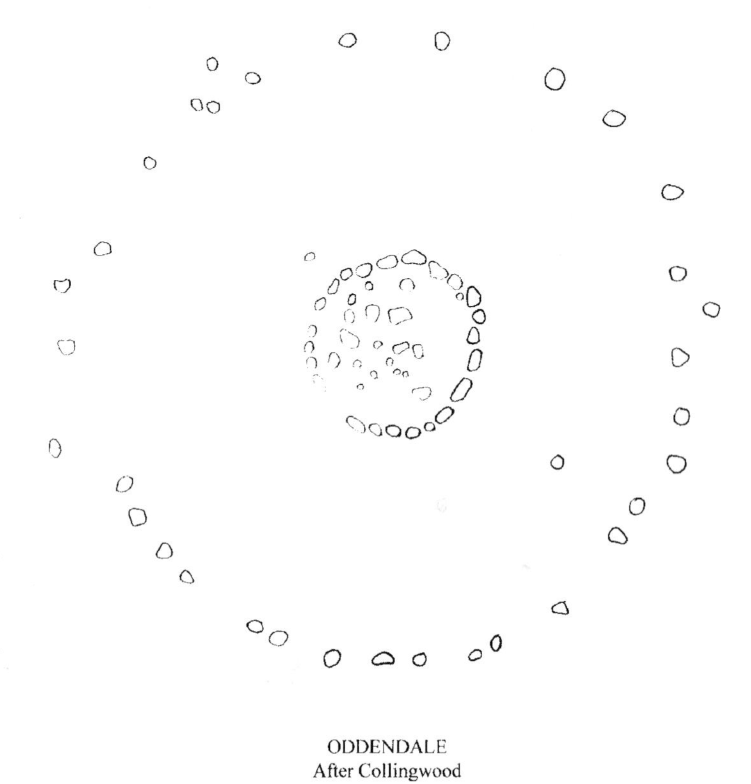

ODDENDALE
After Collingwood

FURTHER READING:

Collingwood, R G, *Prehistoric Settlements near Crosby Ravensworth*, TCWAAS, Volume 33, 1933.

Simpson, J, *The Antiquities of Shap in the County of Westmorland*, Arch. J, Volume 18, 1861.

Simpson, J, *Stone Circles near Shap, Westmorland*, PSAS (1st Series), Volume 4, 1863.

18. Kemp Howe and the Shap Avenue

The remains of Kemp Howe Stone Circle from the S.

DESCRIPTION:

THE NAME Shap means 'a heap of stones', and the local stone is a biotic granite with large crystals of pink. Its distinctive colour may have given the stone a special significance, for it seems to be the most frequently-used stone in the circles of the eastern Lakeland fells. It is difficult to know for sure if this was a single monument or was a group of several individual monuments. Every known archaeological report and survey has struggled to rationalise and make sense of the layout of the monument.

Six stones of Shap granite are all that remain of Kemp Howe. The circle was destroyed by the building of the railway in 1844; the surviving stones lie to the W of the railway embankment. The stones are very large and it must once have been a circle of magnificent proportions, with a diameter thought to have been approximately 24m (80ft). The circle was at the southern terminus of what was one of the finest megalithic monuments in Cumbria, the Shap Avenue, once described as a 'stupendous monument of antiquity', consisting of 'two lines of huge obelisks of unhewn granite'. The avenue consisted of a double row of stones commencing at Kemp Howe 2.4km (1.5m) S of Shap and extending in a northerly direction.

The first detailed account of the monument dates to the visit of the antiquarian William Stukeley in 1725. Stukeley had the monument surveyed but this unfortunately has not survived. Stukeley describes what was an avenue 21.3m (70ft) wide 'composed of very large

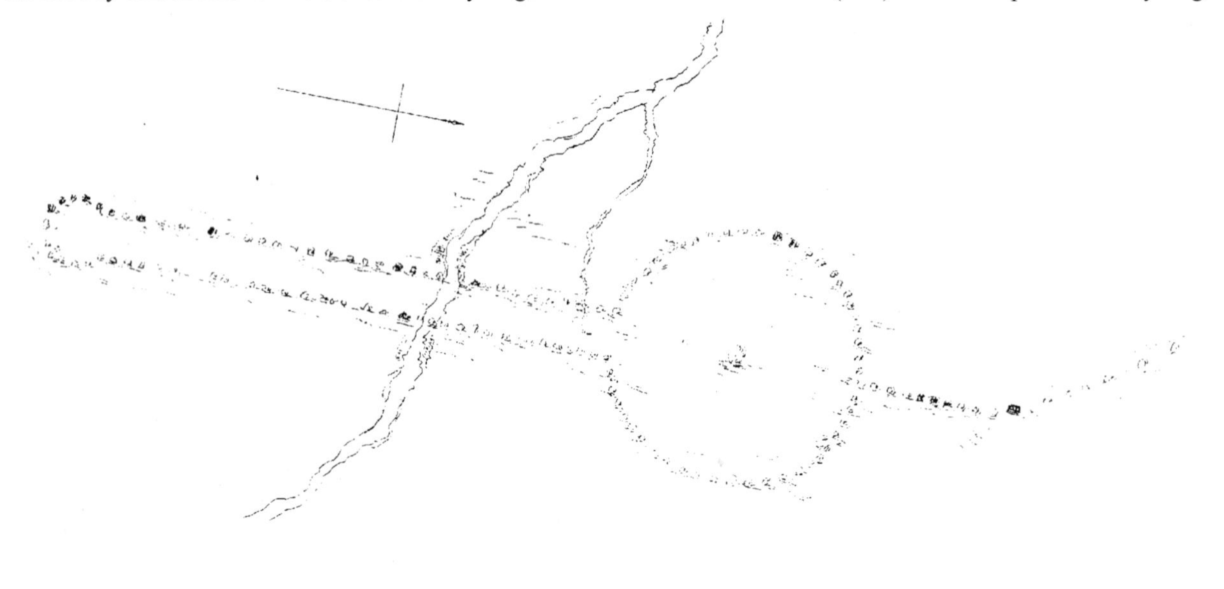

PLATE III.

SHAP STONES.

Ground Plan, suggested by Dr. Simpson.

Kemp Howe and Shap Avenue from a drawing by Dr Simpson.

GRID REF:
Kemp Howe Stone Circle NY 5680 1330;
Stone SW of Brakenber Farm NY 5666 1409;
Stone at Green Farm – NW of the Greyhound Hotel NY 5659 1427;
Stone behind the King's Arms NY 5629 1478;
Stone NE of Peggy Wood NY 5605 1496;
The Goggleby Stone NY 5592 1509;
Stone in Asper's Field NY 5584 1520;
Stone E of Keld Lane NY 5555 1526;
Stone in wall E of Keld Lane NY 5554 1528;
Skellaw Hill NY 5564 1547; The Thunder Stone NY 5515 1573.

ELEVATION: Kemp Howe Stone Circle 265m (869ft).

MAP: OS Explorer (1:25000) OL5; OS Landranger (1:50000) 90.

LOCATION: Kemp Howe Stone Circle Latitude N 54.30.791; Longitude WO 02.40.122; 2km (1.25 miles) S of Shap on the A6:
Stone SW of Brakenber Farm Latitude N 54.31.219; Longitude WO 02.40.255:
Stone at Green Farm – NW of the Greyhound Hotel Latitude N 54.31.314; Longitude WO 02.40.329:
Stone behind the King's Arms Latitude N 54.31.587; Longitude WO 02.40.605:
Stone NE of Peggy Wood Latitude N 54.31.674; Longitude WO 02.40.842:
The Goggleby Stone Latitude N 54.31.753; Longitude WO 02.40.952:
Stone in Asper's Field Latitude N 54.31.814; Longitude WO 02.41.032:
Stone E of Keld Lane Latitude N 54.31.845; Longitude WO 02.41.296:
Stone in wall E of Keld Lane Latitude N 54.31.850; Longitude WO 02.41.306:
Skellaw Hill Latitude N 54.31.955; Longitude WO 02.41.213:
The Thunder Stone Latitude N 54.32.092; Longitude WO 02.41.680.

PARKING: A car park is located off the A6 opposite Shap Methodist Chapel in the centre of the village.

WALKING DISTANCE: From the village centre to Kemp Howe 2.1km (1.3m). From Skellaw Hill to Kemp Howe 2.5 3km (1.5 1.8m).

TERRAIN: Pasture.

stones, set at equal intervals: it seems to be closed at this end which is on an eminence and near a long flattish barrow, with some works upon it; hence it proceeds northward to the town, which intercepts the continuation of it...' this end refers to Kemp Howe. He then goes on to describe the northern progression of the monument stating that the avenue '... makes a very large curve, or arc of a circle, as those at Abury, and passes over a brook too. A spring likewise arises in it, near the Greyhound Inn. By the brook is a little round Sacellum, composed of twelve stones, but lesser ones, set by one great stone belonging to the side of the Avenue; the interval of the stones is 35ft, half the breadth of the avenue; the stones no doubt did all stand upright...' from here '...it ascends the hill, crosses the common road to Penrith, and so goes into corn-fields on the other side of the way westwards, where some stones are left standing; one particularly called Goggleby stone.'

A later account by Dr Simpson, who was vicar of Shap from 1857 to 1863, differs dramatically from Stukeley's in certain details. He stated that the avenue connected Kemp Howe stone circle with a far larger one to the N at Brackenber or Brackenbyre; the stones SW of Brackenber Farm and NW of the Greyhound Hotel are possible survivors of this monument.

This circle, with a large stone at its centre, was 122m (400ft) in diameter, some 12-29m (40-95ft) larger than Long Meg and her Daughters; it would therefore have been the largest stone circle in Cumbria. The plan (opposite page) is that suggested in a drawing by Simpson.

Then the avenue continued to the N, terminating in the vicinity of

DETAILED DIRECTIONS:
A public footpath beside the road leads from the village to the remains of the circle near the railway embankment E of the A6. The circle can be seen from the footpath. Private land. A network of paths to the W of the A6 allows access to the surviving stones of the avenue. For the stone behind the King's Arms take the Public Footpath to the S of the Inn. For the Goggleby Stone follow the Public Footpath for Keld off West Close behind the Fire Station. The Keld Lane public footpath is in the vicinity of signage for Shap Abbey on the Shap – Bampton road.

Skellaw Hill where a tumulus is to be found. Somewhere in the region of Skellaw Hill the avenue then seems to have extended in a NW direction for a further 600m (2000ft). It has proven difficult to ascertain whether this change of direction was to avoid Skellaw Hill, or whether this feature was a different avenue, it may alternatively reflect a knowledge of a visual orientation.

From the vicinity of the Goggleby stone at midsummer solstice the sun sets on the western edge of Knipescar to the N, on an azimuth approximately defined by the Thunder Stone to the N of High Buildings Farm. This suggests that the summer solstice may have had some significance to the orientation of the northern section of the avenue.

The most important parts of the avenue to survive must be the Goggleby stone, the stone in Asper's Field and the tumulus on Skellaw Hill, all of which align upon the unconventional stone circle on Knipescar Common (see the Knipescar Common Stone Circles). Recently an archaeologist has likened the appearance of the Scar to a giant long barrow when seen from the south. At 342m (1122ft) in height Knipescar is a conspicuous land feature which can be seen from Kemp Howe. This may have been a contributing factor in choosing to terminate the northen avenue visually on the Scar, perceiving the land form to be an ancient sacred place. This also may strengthen the tradition which claims that the avenue continued as far as the Kop Stone on Moor Divock.

The avenue does seem to project its presence further into the landscape than the evidence of its remains would suggest. The destruction of the stone avenue commenced as early as 1777, when it was recorded that many of the stones were being blasted and carried away for the foundations of buildings.

A watercolour based on a sketch by Lady Lowther just two years prior to this gives us a rare glimpse of the stone circle and avenue in all its lost glory, with the circle, then known as Shapsey, in the foreground and the avenue winding into the distance. The quiet country lane that can be seen alongside the avenue is now the busy A6. We can be sure that the portrayal is accurate because the remaining stones of Kemp Howe in the foreground are still recognisable. Here at Kemp Howe the circle and the southern part of the avenue were located on a low ridge between two valleys.

By 1824 enclosure was causing much destruction, and the construction of the railway completed the process. Many of the stones must have been recycled in the foundations of walls, road and houses, now incorporated into the fabric of the village. Indeed the village we see today has been shaped by the avenue's linearity, and the ghostly presence of the avenue lies at its heart. In a map of the railway made a few years after its completion, the stone circle is shown to extend on both sides of the embankment. Only the stones to the W can now be seen; it is thought that the stones to the E were removed in the 1960s, when the sidings for the quarry were built.

From a scrutiny of the drawings it is plain to see that the land to the E of the avenue is undulating, and the levelled area within the avenue would have provided an ideal, ready-made surface for the railway. It would seem that by 1899 there was very little of the circle and avenue remaining.

It has been estimated that there were approximately 500 stones in the avenue. The Ordnance Survey and the Royal Commission (1936) recorded nine stones, besides the Thunder Stone, the sole remains of the avenue, although a survey in the 1970s suggested a possible 27 surviving remains. Remnants of stone which may have once belonged to the avenue can be seen the length and breadth of the village – many in the footings of dry stone walls.

The major remains of this once-impressive

megalithic complex which survive now can all be reached by a series of footpaths. Starting from the S these remains are: Kemp Howe stone circle; a stone to the NW of the Greyhound Hotel, W of the A6; a huge stone behind the Kings Arms; another huge stone, the full height of the wall N of Peggy Wood; the largest survivior, known as the Goggleby stone; a stone in alignment in Asper's Field between the Goggleby stone and the tumulus on Skellaw Hill (The Hill of Skulls); and finally the Thunder Stone.

A large stone can also be seen in the wall below Skellaw Hill which is also in alignment with the Goggleby stone, the Asper's Field stone and the hill. For an alternative, route start at Skellaw Hill, easily reached by following the road N of the village to Shap Abbey, and then journey southwards. A comparison of the features of the avenue with that of other surviving avenues and alignments elsewhere would suggest a late Neolithic date.

FURTHER READING:

Clare, T, *Recent Work on the Shap "Avenue"*, TCWAAS, Volume 78, 1978.

Ferguson, R. S, *Shap Stones*, CW I, Volume 15, 1899.

Lukis, W C, *Shap Avenue, Westmorland*, PSAL 10, 1894.

Simpson, J, *The Antiquities of Shap in the County of Westmorland.*, Arch. J, Volume 18, 1861.

The Goggleby Stone.

19. The Kirk

The Kirk from the W.

GRID REF:
SD 2507 8269.

ELEVATION:
205m (672ft).

MAP:
OS Explorer (1:25000) OL6;
OS Landranger (1:50000) 96.

LOCATION:
Latitude N 54.14.067;
Longitude WO 03.09.065:
5.5km (3.5m) NW of Ulverston,
2km (1.2m) E of
Kirkby in Furness.

PARKING:
Restricted, before
Low Ghyll House.

WALKING DISTANCE:
1km (0.6m).

TERRAIN:
Moor.

DESCRIPTION:
THE KIRK is located upon Long Moor, slightly below a rise from where there are magnificent views of the Duddon Sands and the estuary to Millom in the distance. The site is surrounded by low fells from the N to the SW and is overlooked by the turbines of a wind farm from the N to ENE. The aspect is mainly open from the SW through to the NW with the heights of Black Combe to the WNW. Immediately to the S of the enclosure the land slopes steeply to Gill House Beck.

The Kirk is approximately circular (somewhat resembling an upturned saucer), consisting of a bank of earth and stone varying in width from 5 to 8m (16-26ft), with a height of about 0.4m (1.3ft), and surrounding a level inner area of approximately 20m (65.6ft). The inner bank has been lined with slabs of stone though very few are visible.

It was reported that large stones once stood along the bank, and some of the hollows that can be seen in the bank may be evidence of the location of these stones. The stones were too conveniently placed, it seems, on this isolated fell, and were used for building material.

To the NE of the circle there is a group of standing stones which might be associated with the circle. It has been suggested that these seem to form two intersecting avenues, one in

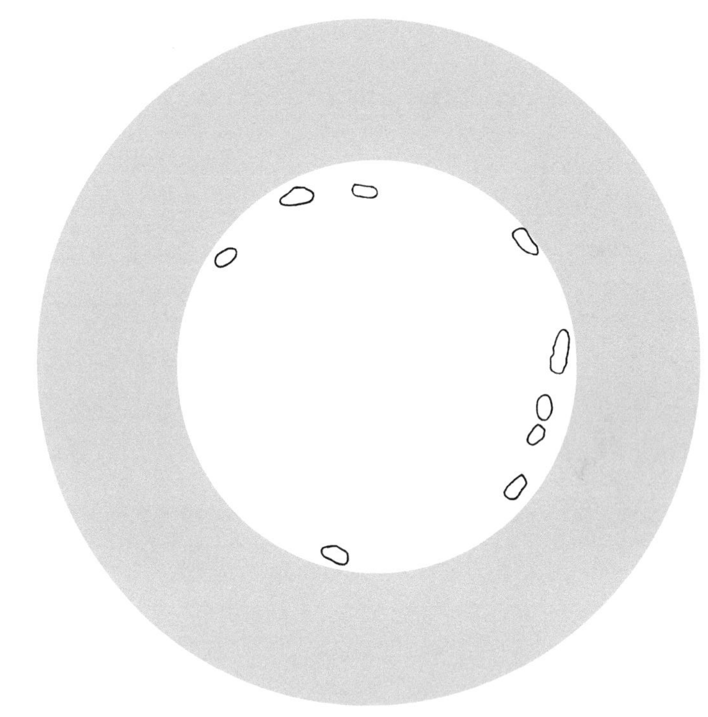

The Kirk - plan drawn by Scruffy Crow.

DETAILED DIRECTIONS:
Turn off the A590-A5092 junction at Grizebeck S for Dalton and Barrow. Continue S to Kirkby in Furness for approximately 4km (2.5m) and turn at the Burlington Inn for Beckside. Continue along the narrow lane, following signs for Low & High Ghyll, for approximately 1.2km (0.8m) to Low Ghyll House. Continue ahead and before the road sweeps round to the right over the bridge take the footpath to the left. Follow the track through a gate to another gate ahead and over a small beck. Follow the grassy track for 130m (435ft) to a public footpath sign, and then bear right along a farm track for 15m (50ft) before turning left along a small grass path in an easterly direction. Continue uphill, keeping Gill House Beck on the right. The grass embankment of the circle is 1.9km (1.2m) from the top of the rise and can soon be clearly seen ahead to the ENE and right of the path.

a NE-SW direction and the other N-S. Supporting this suggestion, the NE-SW avenue does seem to have some astronomical significance in that it aligns with a notch on the horizon where the sun rises at the summer solstice.

It has also been suggested that the N-S avenue is connected to a large cairn higher on the moor, approximately 315m (1,000ft) NNE of the Kirk. However, these features are fairly ruined. The most significant alignment is that to the Great Knott on Lacra Bank which is due west from the centre of the Kirk, where the sun would set at the equinox. This is all the more convincing given the presence of other equinoctial trends at the Lacra circles (see the Lacra Circles).

Tradition records that the Kirk was used on Easter Monday by the lord of the manor and his tenants for games and dancing well into the 19th century, but were discontinued when the last lord to attend broke his thigh during the games. The Kirk has been dated according to an analysis of its traits to the early Bronze Age.

FURTHER READING:

Jopling, C M, *A Letter to George Godwin, Esq. F.R.S, F.S.A. & c. & c. on the Subject of Remains Ascribed to the Era of the Druids in Furness, north of Lancashire*, Arch. Volume 31, 1846.

20. Knipescar Common Stone Circles

DESCRIPTION:

THE WHOLE scar is an isolated high plateau which commands extensive views in every direction, with the steep slopes of Knipescar Common overlooking the villages of Bampton, Bampton Grange and the valley of the River Lowther, looking towards the eastern fells of the Lakes.

On the other side of the valley to the NW just 4km (2.5m) away are the Moor Divock group of monuments. To the E the broad expanse of the megalithic highway of the Eden valley is set against the high Pennine fells. If the site of Knipescar wasn't marked by a stake, it would be easily missed. The circle once known as the Druids' Circle is well-camouflaged, consisting of a circle of limestone boulders amongst an area of limestone pavement. Many of the stones appear to have been cleared from the central area to form a continuous bank of stone. Almost in the centre of the circle is a large boulder of limestone measuring approximately 1.2 by 0.9m (4 by 3ft), the axis of the boulder lying approximately N-S.

The circle is on a gentle incline which slopes to the E, giving some protection from the prevailing winds at this exposed site. The immediate horizon is approximately 65m (213ft) away and most of the eastern fells are effectively hidden just below it. Standing on the central boulder is enough to open up the view including the distinctive saddle of Blencathra just showing above the horizon to the WNW. The wooden stake has been placed conveniently in alignment with the central boulder and Blencathra.

The circle has an approximate diameter of 14.6m (48ft), and it has been reported that there was an entrance to the SE about 1.8m (6ft) wide, although this is not so apparent now.

Knipescar does not conform to the accepted definition of a stone circle and herein may lie its importance – did location take priority over tradition? The circle is

GRID REF:
Knipe Scar Stone Circle
NY 5288 1930;
Tumulus NY 5318 1943.

ELEVATION:
328m (1076ft).

MAP:
OS Explorer (1:25000) OL5;
OS Landranger (1:50000) 90.

LOCATION:
Knipescar Stone Circle
Latitude 54.34.005;
Longitude 02.43.817:
Tumulus Latitude 54.34.078;
Longitude 02.43.532:
5km (3.25m):
5.25km (3.2m) NW of Shap
and 11km (7m) S of Penrith.

PARKING:
Bampton Grange.

WALKING DISTANCE:
2.9km (1.8m).

TERRAIN:
Steep hillside, grassy fell,
limestone pavement.

almost equidistant between the two major groups of Kemp Howe and the Shap Avenue to the S and the Moor Divock stone circles to the NW. It seems that the location of Knipescar may also have some significance to the Shap Avenue (see Kemp Howe and the Shap Avenue).

There are other prehistoric remains to be seen nearby. Within the plantation there is an enclosure, and beyond the trees there are several tumuli on the scar side to the E. The whole area is littered with a confusion of remains but of most interest is the prominent tumuli, which can be seen on the skyline some 200m (660ft) ESE from the gate, which allows access from the plantation onto the scar side. Seen from the E this tumulus is in alignment with the summit of Great Mell Fell and the saddle of Blencathra, echoing a similar alignment seen at the nearby Cockpit stone circle on Moor Divock (see The Moor

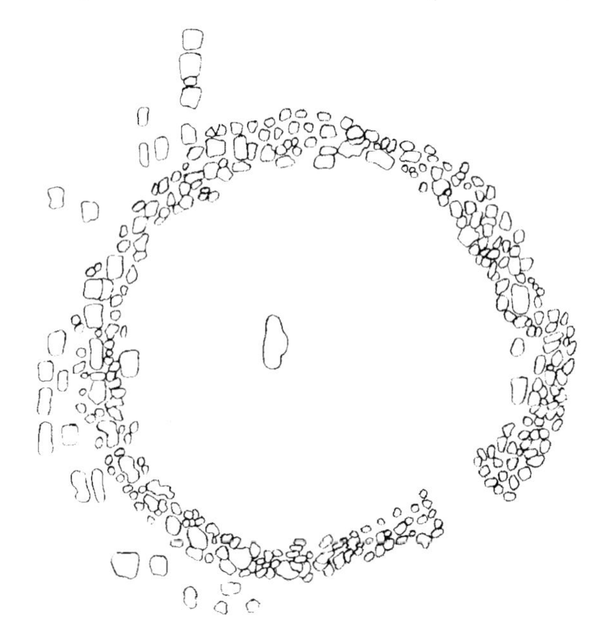

Knipescar Stone Circle

DETAILED DIRECTIONS:
Take the minor road E of Bampton Grange for Knipe and Whale, passing the cemetery on the left. After the cattle grid take the signposted public footpath to the right, following the line of the dry stone wall. At the corner of the wall turn sharp left along the foot of the hill. This leads to a broader path which leads uphill through gorse, towards another field system. Howgate Foot can be seen in the valley to the left.

At the corner of the dry stone wall High Knipe Farm comes into view. Take the path towards the farm, keeping the dry stone wall on your left. Nearing the farm leave the wall and take the broad grassy track bearing right uphill towards another dry stone wall. Follow the steep path along the wall which leads uphill towards the scar. Eventually this wall joins a wall enclosing a plantation. Here a gate can be seen which will give access to the scar side. However, to proceed first to Knipescar, bear right along the path which follows the outside of the wall enclosing the plantation, heading in a southerly direction.

The site of the Knipescar Stone Circle can be seen marked by a stake to the right of the path. After visiting Knipescar, backtrack to the gate and into the plantation. Turn right along faint paths uphill through an enclosure keeping close to the northern side of the plantation. After approximately 250m (800ft) a gate on the northern side of the plantation comes into view which allows access to the scar side; from here a tumulus can be seen ESE. Bear right through a gate immediately ahead onto the scar.

To continue from the cairn to Shapbeck stone circle (see Shapbeck Stone Circle) approximately 2.35km (1.4m) distant, head SE between the two groups of trees towards a tree plantation on the horizon. A large megalithic waymark comes into view. Take the broad grassy bridleway to the left along Out Scar, skirting Shap Quarry to the S. The bridleway leads through a plantation to farmland with one of the finest views of Shapbeck stone circle immediately ahead.

Divock Stone Circles and Castlerigg). From here Great Mell Fell resembles a giant round barrow and perhaps this was its significance to those who built the smaller barrow on the scar.

Just below the summit of Knipescar to the SE was the Wilson Scar stone circle (NY 549 182), which was accurately surveyed and excavated prior to the site being demolished due to the expansion of Shap Quarry in 1952. The circle was located on a slight slope below the crest of the Scar whcih meant that although the views to the N were restricted, to the S the views would have been extensive. The circle consisted of 35 stones, all local erratics, with a diameter of 18.3m (60ft), which had been placed at level ground. All the stones were prostrate 'on their longest sides in their natural resting positions'. When excavated they were shown to be fairly uniform in size and shape measuring 'up to 1.5 by 1.2m (5 by 4ft) in horizontal dimensions'. The stones were retained by a low external bank of stones which directly abutted the stones of the circle.

Four funerary deposits were found associated with the circle: A compact black mass of bone fragments suggesting it came from the interior of an 'urn, or small funerary pit' from the NE quadrant; an inhumation from the centre of the circle, which it is thought may have been the primary burial; a partial cremation; and a complete interment, where all the major skeletal parts were found just below the turf close to the edge of the circle in the NW quadrant. This group of monuments, together with Shapbeck stone circle, suggests that Knipescar Common was of considerable importance during the period of the Bronze Age.

FURTHER READING:

Noble, M, *The Stone Circle on Knipe Scar*, TCWAAS (New Series), Volume 7, 1907.

Sieveking, G. De G, *Excavation of a Stone Circle at Wison Scar, Shap North*, TCWAAS (New Series), Volume 52, 1953.

Simpson, J, *Stone Circles near Shap,* TCWAAS (Old Series), Volume 6, 1883.

Simpson, J, *Stone circles near Shap, Westmorland*, PSAS (1ST Series), Volume 4, 1863.

Spence, J E, *A Stone Circle in Shap Rural Parish*, TCWAAS (New Series), Volume 35, 1935.

21. The Lacra Circles

The Giant's Grave.

DESCRIPTION:

THE GIANT'S GRAVE consists of two stones and is appropriately named being amongst the tallest stones in Cumbria. The stones are almost identical, two tall thin slabs measuring 2m (6.5ft) and 3m (9.8ft) and stand 4.5m (14.7ft) apart. The unhewn stones also share a similar axis to the NW. Standing between the stones the hill of the Lacra circles is due E, and the sun rises above the hill at the equinox. There also appears to be equinoctial features in the placing of the stones on the hill.

Lacra can be described as the first and last fell in Cumbria, and because of this commands extensive sea views. The stones of the Lacra circles are located on the southern face of a hill which rises steeply from the coastal plain to the NE of the village of Kirksanton. The views from the hill are well worth the steep climb, looking over Millom and the Hodbarrow Lake Nature Reserve; to the S are the Duddon Sands, with the Whicham Valley and Black Combe to the N.

The circles take the name Lacra from the ruined farmhouse. They are located on level ground, reminiscent of the terraces on the high ridge of the hill. The land was once cultivated and this is possibly why the circles are in such a ruinous condition. The stones of the Lacra circles belong to the Borrowdale Volcanics.

Lacra A consists of eight irregular boulders, ranging from 0.2-1m (0.6-3.2ft) in height and with a diameter of 15.5m (50ft). The track intrudes upon the northern section of the circle where an opening occurs; there

Lacra B.

GRID REF:
The Giant's Grave SD 1362 8109;
Lacra A SD 1498 8132;
Lacra D SD 1511 8125;
Lacra C SD 1492 8098;
Lacra B SD 1492 8098.

ELEVATION:
The Giant's Grave 12m (39.3ft);
Lacra A 145.3m (477ft);
Lacra D 142m (466ft);
Lacra C 125.2m (411ft);
Lacra B 131m (430ft).

MAP: OS Explorer (1:25000) OL6;
OS Landranger (1:50000) 96.

LOCATION:
The Giant's Grave Latitude N 54.13.099; Longitude WO 03.19.099: Lacra A Latitude N 54.13.235; Longitude WO 03.18.325: Lacra D Latitude N 54.13.197; Longitude WO 03.18.198: Lacra C Latitude N 54.13.047; Longitude WO 03.18.292: Lacra B Latitude N 54.13.050; Longitude WO 03.18.374: 1km (0.6m) ENE of Kirsanton and 2.5km (1.5miles) WNW of Millom.

PARKING: In the village of Kirksanton.

WALKING DISTANCE:
The Giant's Grave 0.6km (0.4m);
Lacra A 1.3km (0.8m); Lacra D 1.47km (0.9m);
Lacra C 1.78km (1.1m);
Lacra B 1.89km (1.17m).

TERRAIN: Coastal plain, steep hillside, grassy fell, wide moor path.

is also a gap in the SW. On a clear day the Isle of Man can be seen to the W. Lacra D can be seen to the E of Lacra A, and the track passes through the site. There seems to be two circles either side of the track. The largest, to the E of the track, has a large flat stone in the centre with several stones in an elliptical setting measuring 18m (59ft) N to S and 15m (50ft) transversely.

An inverted cinerary urn was found at the base of one of the stones. Although the upper section was intact, the base of the urn had been damaged possibly when the field was under cultivation. This main circle lies due S of Great Knott, the summit of the hill. To the W of the track there is a curved setting of stones which indicates a diameter of 5m (16ft); this too appears to have a central stone. It has been suggested that both these central stones have the appearance of being cap-stones belonging to cists.

There appears to be the remains of an avenue of ten stones, approximately 47m (155ft) ENE from the main circle; some of these are in pairs. This

Lacra A

DETAILED DIRECTIONS:
For the Giant's Grave take the lane heading S past the King William IV Public House, pass Manor Farm to the left. As the lane bends to the left take the public footpath toward Standing Stones Farm. At the farm take the stile to the right, the Giant's Grave standing stones can be seen ahead to the NNE 120m (390ft) distant.

For the Lacra stone circles head E past the village green for approximately 45m (150ft) and take the Public Footpath to the left for Po House, crossing the railway line. Head uphill following the line of the dyke towards the partly restored ruin of a farmhouse to the NNE on the saddle between the two hills. At the farm go through the old farmyard past the farmhouse and take the NE exit out of the yard and onto the fell – a wide track leads to the Lacra 'A' stone circle, which is 90m (300ft) E of the farmhouse. Continue along the track ESE to the Lacra 'D' complex approximately 150m (500ft) from Lacra 'A'. Lacra 'C' and Lacra 'B' can just be seen to the S. From Lacra 'D' continue SSW keeping to the outside of the wall along its full length; Lacra 'C' can be seen directly S from the corner of the wall. From Lacra 'C' head W/N for 91.4m (300ft) for Lacra 'B' which is hidden by the higher foreground.

FURTHER READING:
Dixon, J A and Fell, C I, *Some Bronze Age Burial Circles at Lacra, near Kirksanton*, TCWAAS, Volume 48, 1948.
Eccleston, J, *Ancient Remains at Lacra and Kirksanton*, TCWAAS (Old Series), Volume 1, 1874.

Lacra B

avenue also appears to continue in the opposite direction for about 100m (330ft) WSW. From the top end of the avenue at an elevation of 146m (480ft) the whole of the Isle of Man is visible to the W and the views extend to the E over the Duddon Sands. The outlook gradually diminishes towards the lower end of the avenue with the Isle of Man hidden completely behind the near horizon.

Only three stones remain of Lacra C but they form part of the SE arc of the original circle and indicate that the circle must have once had a diameter of 24m (78ft). A fourth stone close to the outcrop of rock to the N is possibly part of the northern arc of the circle. From here, in clear conditions, the Irish coast can be seen to the SSW and a line of sight from the summit of Great Knott through Lacra D to Lacra C aligns on this.

Six stones remain of Lacra B, which closely resembles Lacra A in both height and diameter but which is slightly smaller at 14.7m (48ft). Lacra B is the most perfect of the Lacra circles and also affords a better all round panorama than the others. The Isle of Man is due W and was indeed an Other-world island of legend, lying in the region of the setting sun. From Lacra A and B, the sun sets over the island at the equinox. The isle lies at the hub of one of Europe's most important megalithic regions, central to southern Scotland, Cumbria, North Wales and eastern Ireland.

During the excavation of Lacra B in 1947 it was shown that some of the surviving stones from the eastern arc of the circle were equidistant from each other. This suggested the possibility that some five stones had gone missing, and these, it is thought, were removed alternately to allow for the passage of a plough when the land was under cultivation. A low mound of 9m (29.5ft) diameter had once been constructed inside the circle and beneath the centre were found pieces of burnt bone from a burial. The Lacra circles suggest a period in time ranging from the early to middle Bronze Age.

Detail of Lacra B with the Isle of Man on the horizon.

22. Leacet Hill

Leacet Hill Stone Circle from the SE

DESCRIPTION:
THE CAIRN circle is located to the W and at the foot of Leacet Hill, which belongs to a range of isolated and prominent high ground within the Eden Valley. The ruinous dry stone wall and the accompanying wire fence runs through the centre of the circle. The wall follows a boundary line which is also a boundary wall of the plantation. Ancient monuments were often used as landmarks for boundaries, which were divided at the time of enclosure. Enclosure resulted in the damage and loss of much that was of archaeological importance.

One way of accounting for the cairn's location is to assume that it was positioned to herald the Mayburgh – Blencathra orientation to the equinox sunset. Mayburgh Henge is just 4.8km (3m) from here and can be seen quite clearly from the top of the hill. Both locations seem to show a common interest in the same horizon event, which seems significant. Although the cairn is probably later than Mayburgh we know from evidence at other sites that there was some continuity of use in monuments spanning the Neolithic and Bronze Age periods.

Blencathra can just be glimpsed through the trees, but from the top of the hill the view would have been unhindered and the sunset upon the mountain would have been quite spectacular in its precision. From the summit of the hill the sun would set upon the saddle approximately five days before the vernal equinox at Mayburgh, and at the spring equinox it would start setting upon the western edge of the mountain five days before the true equinox at the Henge.

At the time of the excavation of the circle in 1880 only seven stones were visible, six outside the wall and one within the plantation. During excavation three more stones A, B and C were found buried within the plantation. Only five large stones now remain to the S of the wall. The diameter of the circle surrounding the cairn was approximately 11.5m (38ft) with the tallest surviving stone having a height of 1.25m (4ft).

Melkinthorpe with Leacet Hill (middle distance) and Cross Fell in the background.

GRID REF:
NY 5630 2629.

ELEVATION:
128m (420ft).

MAP:
OS Explorer (1:25000) OL5;
OS Landranger (1:50000) 90.

LOCATION:
Latitude N 54.37.794;
Longitude WO 02.40.702:
6.5km (4miles) SE of Penrith, turn left off the A6 S of Eamont Bridge for Cliburn.

PARKING:
Restricted.

WALKING DISTANCE:
Nearest route 0.4km (0.2m);
Alternative route 1.2km (0.8m).

TERRAIN:
Forestry track, grassy path, rough pathless scrub.

Excavation showed that the site had been used extensively for cremated burial with what was considered the remains of a funeral pyre at the centre, consisting of a layer of charcoal about 30cm (1ft) thick interspersed with fragments of calcined bones and reddened stone. Several vessels were found; five collared urns, a food vessel and a pygmy urn. All had been placed at the base of the stones and all contained cremated bones. At the same time as the excavation of the circle, a mound on top of Leacet Hill was also investigated; this was described as a 'saucer-like place, with a ditch around, like the so called 'pond barrows' but nothing was found.' The finds within the circle suggest a date most probably of the Bronze Age period. More recently some linear and curved features, situated between the N slope of the hill and the S slope of an adjacent hill have been interpreted as an enclosure and possible cremation cemetery dating to the early Bronze Age.

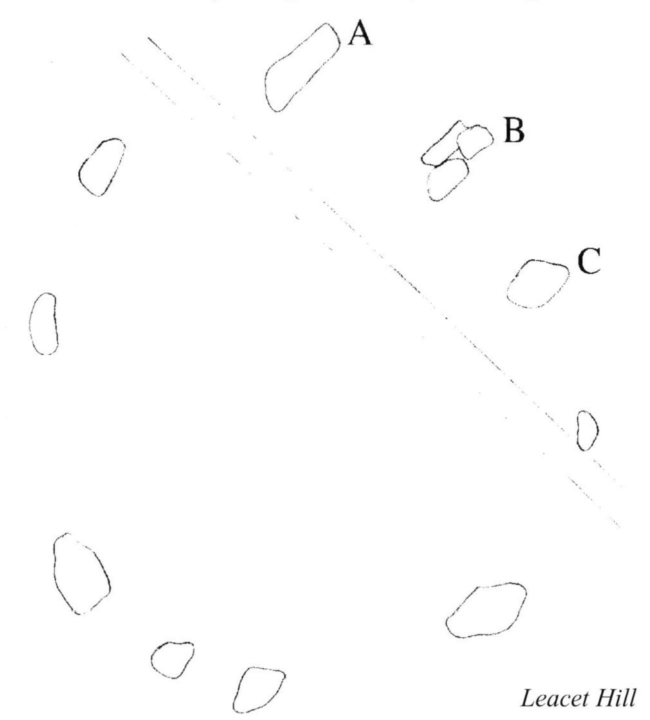

Leacet Hill

DETAILED DIRECTIONS:
The stone circle can be seen from the vicinity of Wetheriggs Pottery at the SW edge of Leacet Hill Plantation. It is on private land owned by the Lowther Estate, and permission is needed for access from the nearest publicly accessible point, which is the forest track opposite the road junction to Melkinthorpe and Lowther. A better alternative is to take the public footpath to the E marked 'Whinfell Forest A66', which is 0.8km (0.5m) S of the Melkinthorpe–Lowther junction. A tarmac drive leads to a gate to the right of a homestead. Go through this gate and head for a second gate immediately ahead. Follow the way marked 'Footpath', with the dry stone wall to the left. After approximately 60m (200ft) cross a stile in the wall and head uphill towards a stile at the edge of the wood. Take the stile into the wood and then the path immediately left, following the line of the fence, which eventually becomes a rather dilapidated sandstone wall. Just as the forest track dips steeply downhill to the clearing, the stone circle can just be seen to the left of the wall in the foreground, with splendid views of Blencathra in the distance. There is an improvised stile in the wall to the N of the circle.

FURTHER READING:
James, Richard, *A Bronze Age enclosure & cremation cemetery at Leacet Hill, Brougham*, TCWAAS, Vol. VI, 2006.
Robinson, J. and Ferguson, R S, *Notes on Excavations at Leacet Hill Stone Circle, Westmorland*, TCWAAS (Old Series), Vol 5, 1881.

23. Little Meg (The Maughanby Stone Circle)

GRID REF:
NY 5769 3747.

ELEVATION:
170m (558ft).

MAP:
OS Explorer (1:25000) OL5;
OS Landranger (1:50000) 91.

LOCATION:
Latitude 54.43.831;
Longitude WO 02.39.509:
10km (6.25miles) NE of Penrith,
on the road from Little Salkeld
to Glassonby approximately
0.5km (0.3m) NE of
Long Meg and her Daughters.

PARKING:
Roadside grass verge.

WALKING DISTANCE:
Negligible.

TERRAIN:
Rutted track at field edge, scrub.

DESCRIPTION:

DUE TO the close vicinity of Long Meg and her Daughters, 650m (2,132.5ft) SW and one of the largest stone circles in Britain, this small and ruined circle is more descriptively known as Little Meg. The monument is also known as the 'Maughanby' (meaning 'Merchiaun's settlement') stone circle. The site is a confusion of stone, possibly owing to its position convenient for field clearance, and there are more stones now than were shown in a plan of 1875.

Little Meg was a kerb-cairn of possibly eleven stones, forming an irregular ring measuring 5.68 by 4.72m (18.6 by 15.4ft) surrounding a mound, which was reported to have partly covered the stones. The size of the stones are impressively large for the diminutive size of the circle, the tallest being over 1m (3.2ft) in height. The gem of Little Meg is the carved stone to the left of this tallest stone, which is one of the finest in Cumbria. The carving a delicately executed spiral linked into a group of concentric circles, which neatly covers the whole of the stone. There are descriptions and drawings from 1867 of two other decorated stones in the circle. One, on the inner face of a large boulder to the E, had an almost mirror-image of the existing rock carving, but about twice the size. This would have been a very impressive carving but is no longer in existence.

Beneath the mound, which was approximately 1.3m (4.2ft) in height, was found a small cist in which was found an urn containing burnt bones and charcoal. Two stones which covered the cist were found to have cup and ring carvings upon them; these marked stones can now be seen in Penrith Museum. An alignment from the centre of Long Meg stone circle through to Little Meg marks the sun rise above Fiend's Fell to the E between the spring equinox and the summer solstice and the summer solstice and the autumn equinox, the Celtic festivals of Beltane (May 1) and Lughnasa (August 1). Remarkably, the line of the field boundary that adjoins Little Meg seems to preserve this line of orientation. The sun would be seen to rise above the gateway to the E, the entrance to the field. It is thought that Little Meg is early Bronze Age. Long Meg could once be seen from Little Meg but the tree plantation now obscures the line of sight.

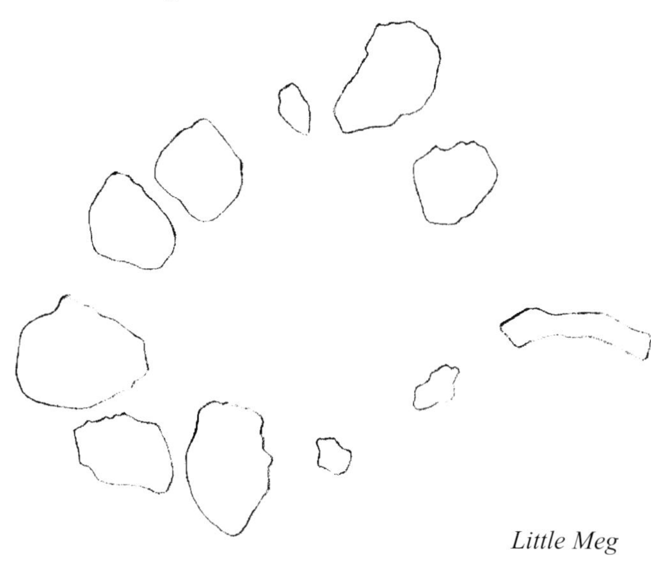

Little Meg

DETAILED DIRECTIONS:
Not signposted. Just N of Tarn House, where an extensive grass verge commences alongside the road. Access is through the gate to the left of the road. The stone circle can be seen from the gate near the edge of the field about 150m (500ft) W, but is often difficult to locate being obscured by long grass during the summer. Private land.

FURTHER READING:

Thornley, W, *Ring-marked Stones at Glassonby and Maughanby*, TCWAAS, Volume 2, 1902.

24. Long Meg and her Daughters

Long Meg in the foreground from the W.

GRID REF:
NY 5711 3721.

ELEVATION:
175m (574ft).

MAP:
OS Explorer (1:25000) OL5;
OS Landranger (1:50000) 91.

LOCATION:
Latitude N 54.43.685;
Longitude WO 02.40.048: 10km (6.2m) NE of Penrith.

PARKING:
Restricted spaces for parking at Long Meg.

WALKING DISTANCE:
None.

TERRAIN:
Pasture.

DESCRIPTION:
LONG MEG and her Daughters is the largest stone circle in Cumbria and the sixth largest in Britain. The circle has a flattened arc in the N giving diameters of 109m (357ft) E-W by 93m (305ft) N-S. The arc adjoins an enormous ditched enclosure, which surrounds the farm; this earthwork, which is over twice the size of the circle, can no longer be seen, although an infra-red aerial photograph shows it clearly. A recent topographical survey shows that the enclosure encompassed the head of a valley which ran down to the Eden and also housed two springs, one in the steep-sided valley and the other within the enclosure. The noticeable slope on which the circle is built is a result of its location at the head of this valley.

The circle now consists of some 69 stones; two of the largest lie approximately E-W,

Long Meg and her Daughters

DETAILED DIRECTIONS:
Signposted off the Little Salkeld to Glassonby road.

FURTHER READING:

Burl, H A W, *The Stone Circle of Long Meg and her Daughters, Little Salkeld*, TCWAAS, Volume 94, 1994.

Clare, T, *Some Cumbrian Stone Circles in Perspective*, TCWAAS, Volume 75, 1975.

Clare, T, *Recent topographical survey of the Long Meg Stone Circle*, Cumbria, 2006

Crawford, O G S, *Long Meg*, Antiquity 8, 1934.

Dymond, C W, *A Group of Cumberland Megaliths*, CW 1 Volume 5, 1881.

Farrah, R W E, *Stones of Power… Raised in Magic Hour*, 3rd Stone, Issue 46, 2003.

Hood, S & Wilson, D, *Long Meg Mid-Winter Shadow Path*, TCWAAS, Third Series, Volume 2, 2002.

Hood, S & Wilson, D, *Further Investigations into the Astronomical Alignments at Cumbrian Prehistoric Sites*, TCWAAS, Third Series, Volume 2, 2003.

Hood, S, *Cumbrian Stone Circles, the Calendar and the Issue of the Druids*, TCWAAS, Third Series, Volume 4, 2004.

Morrow, J, *Sun and Star Observations at the Stone Circles of Keswick and Long Meg*, Proceedings of the University of Durham Philosophical Society, 1909.

Soffe, G & Clare, T, *New Evidence of Ritual Monuments at Long Meg and her Daughters, Cumbria*, Antiquity 62, 1988.

while the largest, to the S, has been estimated to weigh some 28 tonnes. There are traces of a slight bank which is most prominent to the W of the circle, but it is not clear whether this is prehistoric or has resulted from ploughing. The circle is located 1km (0.6m) E of the river Eden, with the northern Lakeland fells to the W and the Pennines dominating the skyline to the E. The land on which the circle was built slopes down towards the N and E, making the stones to the W and S appear more prominent against the skyline. It has been estimated that the NE arc is approximately 6m (20ft) lower than Long Meg.

The focus of the circle is to the SW, where two pairs of stones define an entrance with the tall tapering stone of Long Meg just beyond. This pillar of Triassic sandstone, standing 3m (12.1ft) high, is the only stone of the circle which has been quarried. Its position seems awkward; from the centre of the circle the stone is not central to the portal stones which define the entrance, and this is often cited as evidence to suggest Long Meg predates the circle. A recent geophysics survey has suggested that Long Meg may not have been a solitary outlier but was possibly one of a pair of stones positioned at the entrance to the circle. Its tabular form is smooth on three faces. The stone's long axis aligns to the S on the eastern edge of the distinctive shape of Wild Boar Fell, where a tumulus is to be found near the summit.

Long Meg is thought to mark the position of the setting sun at the winter solstice from the centre of the circle. More recent research has shown that the shadow cast by Long Meg at sunset at the winter solstice strikes the stone to the N and just E, of the road suggesting that the measurement of the shadow path helped determine the circle. This is also strengthened by the fact that the shadow path of Long Meg at Samhain/Imbolc crosses the two SE portal stones before reaching the largest stone in the circle to the E, suggesting that Long Meg not only predated the circle but was instrumental in determining the proportions of it – a gnomon for the seasonal dial of the circle. However, the true azimuth for the winter solstice falls between the neighbouring stones in the NE arc of the circle, stones 2 and 3, E of the road, and this orientation shares certain symbolic traits which seem both familiar and significant. Along this azimuth, from the centre of the circle, Long Meg aligns on the summit of the highest mountain to the SW, Helvellyn, and it is upon the dome of Helvellyn where the sun sets at the winter solstice.

Long Meg in the middle distance from the E.

The NE face of Long Meg has a wealth of carved spirals and concentric rings, which makes the stone one of the finest examples of rock art in Cumbria. There is also mention of another stone circle existing SW of Long Meg on higher ground, thought to have been approximately the same size as the nearby Glassonby stone circle (see Glassonby). This was recorded in a drawing of the monument by the antiquarian William Stukeley on his visit in August 1725. A survey in the 1930s was able to locate the position of this circle in the vicinity of a now-ruined barn. The stones of the circle were possibly used in the construction of the building.

Long Meg from the NE.

Also of interest in Stukeley's drawing is what appears to be a mound to the W within the same field as the circle. The mound looks as if it may have aligned with the largest stone of the circle in the E with the distant mountain of Blencathra.

An infamous incident occurred towards the end of the 18th century, when the owner of the monument, a Lt. Colonel Samuel Lacy, attempted to remove it by blasting. We are told that while the work was proceeding under Lacy's orders, 'the slumbering powers of druidism rose in arms against this violation of their sanctuary; and such a storm of thunder and lightning, and such heavy rain and hail ensued, as the Fell-sides never before witnessed. The labourers fled for their lives, vowing never more to meddle with Long Meg'. It has been suggested that this 'manifestation of the supernatural' was Lacy's very own Road to Damascus.

Prior to this the monument had been divided, a ditch having been cut across the circle from E to W, the northern half had been ploughed, while the southern half remained as common land. It is recorded that at this time 'the fences of the fields intersected it, so that from no quarter a proper view of the whole circle could be had'. Lacy, 'to gratify the curious', set about removing those obstacles in a process of restoration. Lacy also commissioned a painting of the monument, *The Druids Cutting Mistletoe* by Jacob Thompson, signed and dated 1832 and exhibited at the Royal Academy in either 1832 or 1833. The name of Long Meg is thought to derive from a Long Meg of Westminster whose adventures in the 16th century were celebrated in pamphlets and plays. This cannot be proven, but in medieval times the description 'Long', meaning tall, was applied to people who were very tall and thin.

Other traditions concerning the stones have it that Long Meg and her Daughters were a coven of witches, who were turned to stone when they were caught holding their sabbat. A similar legend states that they were turned to stone for profaning the Sabbath with wild dancing. A magic which prevails at the stones is supposed to make it impossible to count the same number of stones twice, and if anyone is successful then it is said Long Meg and her coven of witches will come back to life, or the devil may appear. This tradition may merely be a threat to anyone taking an interest in a pre-Christian monument at a time when fear of witchcraft and magic was real.

Long Meg has many features which suggests an early date for the circle, such as a single entrance with portal stones, an outlier and a large open area, traits which suggest a middle to late Neolithic date, making it one of the first to have been built in Cumbria.

25. Mayburgh and King Arthur's Round Table

Mayburgh from the E.

GRID REF:
Mayburgh NY 5192 2842:
King Arthur's Round Table
NY 5233 2838.

ELEVATION:
Mayburgh 130m (426.5ft):
King Arthur's Round Table
120m (394ft).

MAP:
OS Explorer (1:25000) OL5;
OS Landranger (1:50000) 90.

LOCATION:
Mayburgh
Latitude N 54.38.921;
Longitude WO 02.44.798:
King Arthur's Round Table
Latitude N 54.38.898;
Longitude WO 02.44.415:
2km (1.25miles) S of Penrith

PARKING:
Layby on A6 opposite King Arthur's Round Table and a layby at Mayburgh Henge.

WALKING DISTANCE:
Negligible

TERRAIN:
Pasture.

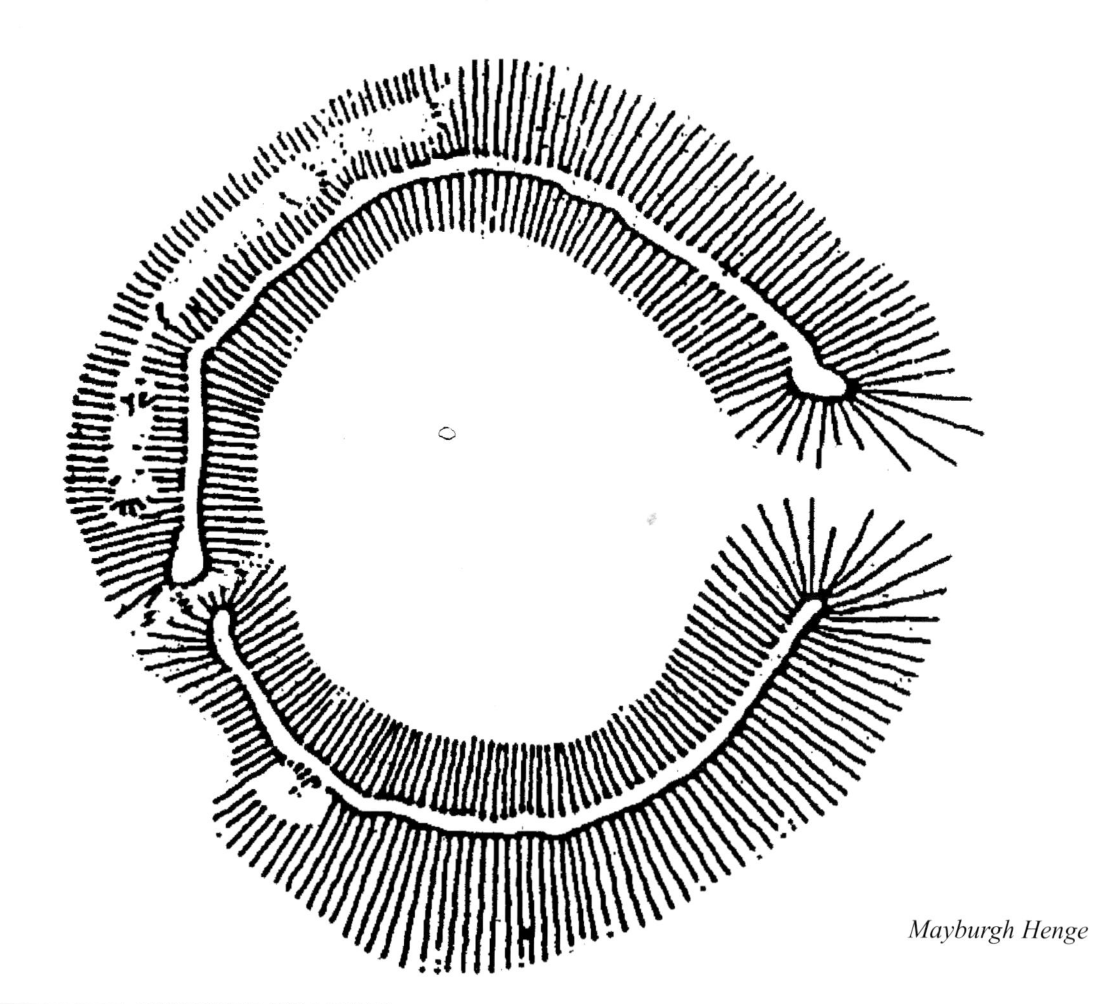

Mayburgh Henge

DETAILED DIRECTIONS:
Both monuments are signposted off the A6 at Eamont Bridge, just south of Penrith.

FURTHER READING:

Atkinson, W, O*n Some Earthworks near Eamont Bridge*, TCWAAS, 1st Series, 6, 1883.
Dymond, C W, *Mayburgh and King Arthur's Round Table*, TCWAAS, 1st Series 2, 1891.
Farrah, R W E, *Mayburgh Henge: A Sacred Space Odyssey*, Northern Earth 85, 2001.
Farrah, R W E, *The Solar Orientation of Mayburgh Henge*, The Matterdale Historical and Archaeological Society Year Book and Transactions, Volume 9, 2002.
Topping, P, *The Penrith Henges: A Survey by the Royal Commission on the Historical Monuments of England*, Proc. Prehistoric Society 58, 1992.

DESCRIPTION:

HENGES ARE earthen banked enclosures with an inner ditch and one or more entrances. They are thought to pre-date or be contemporary with the earliest stone circles which may have evolved from them.

The henges at Eamont Bridge were once a group of three, which are collectively known as the Penrith Henges. All three are clearly illustrated in drawings by the early antiquarians Stukeley (1725) and Pennant (1769). They are located within 155m (508ft) of each other, between the River Eamont to the N and its tributary the Lowther to the S.

The smallest of the three, known as the Little Round Table, has virtually disappeared and its authenticity has been doubted. It was located 75m (250ft) S of King Arthur's Round Table, which is the only true henge by definition, and is located on a river terrace.

The northern entrance of King Arthur's Round

King Arthur's Round Table with Mayburgh in the background among the trees.

Table and the E banks of the monument have now disappeared beneath roads, but the southern entrance which was opposite the northern entrance still survives. The outside of the northern entrance was distinguished by two large portal stones. These were recorded in a drawing by Sir William Dugdale in the 16th century. The henge bank ranges from about 10-13m (33-43ft) across and has a height of 0.5-2m (1.6-6.5ft). The bank encloses a ditch which has a width ranging from 12.5-16m (41-52ft), with an approximate depth of 1.6m (5.2ft). The ditch surrounds an elliptical platform varying from 44-52m (144-170ft) in diameter. It has been suggested that there may have been a central prehistoric mound.

In 1820 the commercial interests of William Bushby the owner of the public house opposite the henge decided to turn the monument into a tea garden. To effect this transformation the inner face of the bank was cut away and the ditch deepened to raise the central area - the 'disc' like feature at the centre has resulted from these alterations.

Mayburgh Henge can be seen from King Arthur's Round Table about 350m (1150ft) to the W, located on an elevated knoll against the skyline. The river cliff to the W of King Arthur's Round Table veils the view of Mayburgh which only comes fully into view around the centre of the Round Table. Mayburgh is almost perfectly circular, with a bank built entirely of millions of water-worn cobbles probably taken from the nearby Eamont; these can be seen exposed in several places along the embankment, beneath the turf.

The bank has a height of 4.5-6.5m (15-21ft) and a width of 35-45m (115-148ft), with an internal area measuring 90m (295ft) N-S by 87.5m (287ft), and with an entrance to the E. It has been estimated that a labour

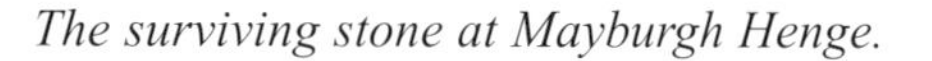

The surviving stone at Mayburgh Henge.

force of about one thousand men would have taken approximately six months to build the enormous banks of the henge. Another feature of Mayburh's banks seen from both N and S of the monument is how the top height of the banks maintain a constant level regardless of the undulating nature of the ground the henge is built upon. There is one surviving stone of what was once a setting of four at the centre of the henge, with two fur ther stones just outside the entrance; these were also recorded by Dugdale.

The surviving stone has a height of 2.7m (9ft) and is located 10m (33ft) NW of the centre. The axis of Mayburgh is aligned E-W. At the equinox the sun rises in the entrance to the E and sets on the centre of the saddle of the distant mountain of Blencathra in the W. The now destroyed N entrance to King Arthur's Round Table would have been the position from which the first frontal elevation of Mayburgh would have been seen, for this coincides with the axis of the solar equinoctial orientation. This is now best viewed from near the entrance of the haulage yard in Mayburgh Close to the E of Mayburgh (opposite King Arthur's Round Table). This event is one of the most visually dramatic solar orientations at a megalithic monument. On a clear day the saddle of the mountain can be seen spanning the bowl of Mayburgh's entrance.

There are some design features common to both henges. Mayburgh's eastern entrance and the northern entrance of King Arthur's Round Table were both distinguished with portal stones. The banks of both monuments also increased in height towards these entrances. Whether by design or not the external bank of King Arthur's Round Table fits inside the interior of Mayburgh's banks.

Blencathra seems to have been the focus of ritual interest for other nearby monuments; Castlerigg 24km (14.9m) W; the Cockpit stone circle 7.2km (4.4m) SW, the tumulus on Knipescar Common 9km (5.5m) S, Leacet Hill stone circle 4.8km (3m) SE and Swarth Fell stone circle 11km (6.8m) SW (see Castlerigg, The Moor Divock Stone Circles, The Knipescar Common Stone Circles, Leacet Hill and Swarth Fell Stone Circle), possibly suggesting a common kinship and descent.

26. The Moor Divock Stone Circles

The Cockpit Stone Circle from the E.

DESCRIPTION:

MOOR DIVOCK is rich in antiquity, dating to the early Bronze Age. It has been described in a late 19th century survey as a necropolis of mortuary remains, although the remains to be seen on Moor Divock today do not always match this survey. Between the Kopstone and White Raise, approximately 1km (0.6m) to the W, a series of ten monuments were identified, mainly cairn circles forming a serpentine course approximately parallel with the track suggesting that both are contemporary. Many of these circles were linked by a series of stone avenues of various breadths which could be traced for a distance of about 490m (1620ft).

The best-preserved parts of the avenue were to be seen between Moor Divock 4 & 5, and beyond Moor Divock 5, towards White Raise. It is thought that some of these monuments may have been turned into hides for grouse shooting, and it has been suggested that some of these hides bear some resemblance to 'hollow-centred burial cairns'.

The monuments described here are the more easily identifiable, and Moor Divock 4 & 5 retain the order of the original survey. Walking westward, the moor rises towards the peaks of Loadpot Hill and Arthur's Pike in the SW. The vista gradually unfolds, with breathtaking views of Ullswater and the fells of the NW, with the distant saddle of Blencathra beyond the local skyline.

The first site visited can be clearly seen from the moorland road; this is the Kopstone. This single standing stone at 1.65m (5.4ft) high is thought to be the largest survivor from the SSE sector of a stone circle. At the time of the survey a low circular earth embankment enclosing an area 17.3m (57ft) across was all that was left of this circle. Outside the earth embankment was evidence of another circle of stones, about ten to twelve still existing 'in a circumferential position' with a diameter of 23.1m (76ft). A local tradition also states that the Shap avenue extended to it.

The stone is clearly visible from many directions and was likely used to waymark the access to and from

GRID REF:
The Kopstone NY 4959 2160: Moor Divock 4 NY 4940 2195:
Moor Divock 5 NY 4931 2218: White Raise NY 4887 2244:
The Cockpit NY 4827 2223.

ELEVATION:
The Kopstone 315m (1034ft): Moor Divock 4315m (1033.4ft):
Moor Divock 5313m (1027ft): White Raise 327m (1073ft):
The Cockpit 323m (1059.7ft).

MAP:
OS Explorer (1:25000) OL5;
OS Landranger (1:50000) 90.

LOCATION:
The Kopstone Latitude 54.35.227; Longitude WO 02.46.886:
Moor Divock 4 Latitude N 54.35.418;
Longitude WO 02.47.070:
Moor Divock 5 Latitude N 54.35.537;
Longitude WO 02.47.160:
White Raise Latitude N 54.35.675; Longitude WO 02.47.564:
The Cockpit Latitude N 54.35.560; Longitude WO 02.48.120:
SW of Helton, 9km (5.5m) S of Penrith.
3.3km (2m) SE of Pooley Bridge.

PARKING:
Alongside the moorland road SW of Helton and in Pooley Bridge.
Restricted parking at the top of Roehead Lane.

WALKING DISTANCE:
The Kopstone is 256m (840ft) from the moorland road, 4.2km (2.6m) from Pooley Bridge and 2.8km (1.7m) from Roehead Lane.
The Cockpit is 2km (1.2m) from the moorland road, 3.3km (2m) from Pooley Bridge and 1.5km (0.9m) from Roehead Lane.

TERRAIN: Grassy bridlepath, rough pathless moorland, some marsh between White Raise and the Cockpit.

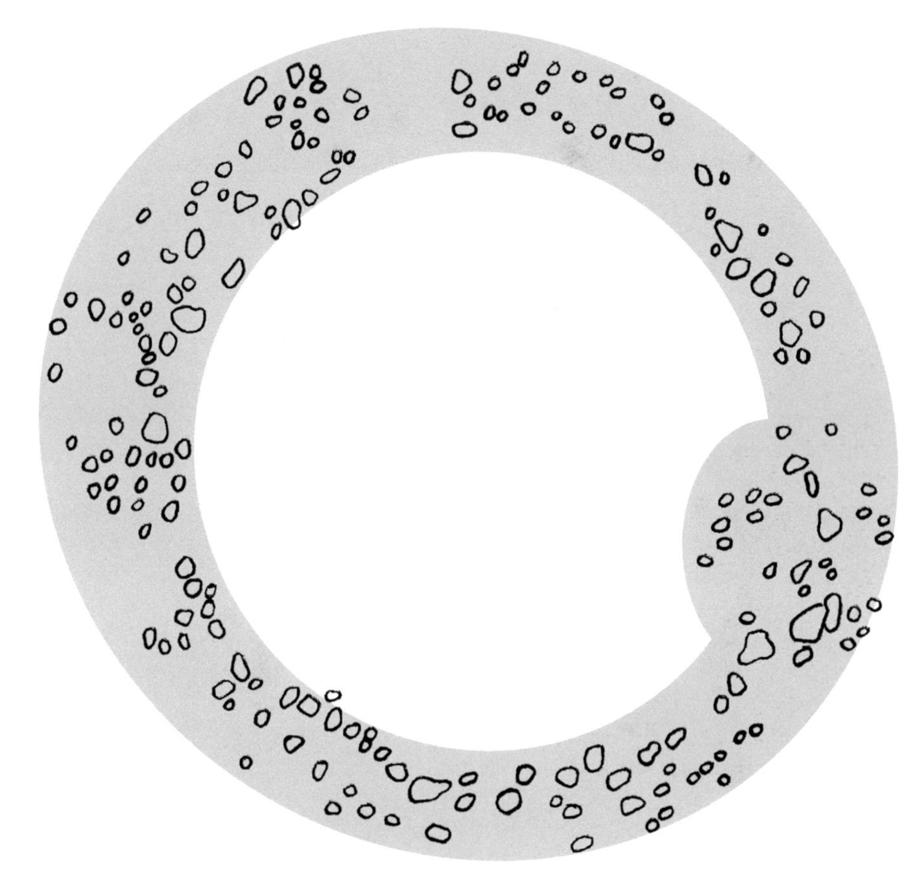

The Cockpit - drawing by Scruffy Crow.

DETAILED DIRECTIONS:
Signposted 'Public Bridleway – Howtown and Pooley Bridge' from the moorland road. Access to Moor Divock is by a broad grassed track which passes close to all the sites mentioned. From Pooley Bridge, walk through the village to the mini roundabout, turn right for Howtown and at the first junction proceed straight ahead up Roehead Lane; access to the moor is from the top of Roehead Lane.

the moor. It is now the eastern terminal of an approximate alignment of circles to the W, Moor Divock 4 and Moor Divock 5. Between the Kopstone and Moor Divock 4 are a distinctive group of boulders and this group of monuments are aligned with the summit of Heughscar Hill. These stones have been described as being part of a 'circle' or 'cromlech' which possibly supported a capstone, the mound measuring some 1.2m high and 4.5m in circumference. From here the midsummer solstice sun would set upon the saddle of Blencathra.

Moor Divock 4 is 440m (1443ft) NW of the Kopstone and is a cairn circle and is also known as 'standing stones'. The cairn has a diameter of 11.5m (38ft) and consists of ten large stones set in a bank around the top of the cairn. Only two of the stones are still standing, and they vary in height from 32-97cm (1-3ft). The cairn was excavated in 1866 and a very fine urn, 14cm (0.4ft) in height, was found beneath the centre of the cairn. The vessel was decorated with a delicate ornamentation consisting of encircling bands of finely twisted cord in a herringbone design, which covered the entire vessel. The urn had been laid on its side with its mouth towards the W in a layer of sand. Beneath this layer was found the burnt bones of an adult.

A short distance to the NW is the more ruinous Moor Divock 5, also a cairn circle. Three large standing stones are all that remain of the cairn, which has an approximate diameter of 14m (46ft). On excavation a collared urn was found at the centre of the cairn opposite the largest of the stones in the NW. The vessel, which was broken and described as being of the 'rudest manufacture', was found to contain a deposit of ashes and burnt bone. The validity of this site's stone circle status has been questioned. The three standing stones form a straight line rather than a curve and are thought to have once formed part of the central cairn, halway between the centre and its perimeter.

Continuing along the track we next come to White Raise. This is the most prominent of the cairns on a slightly elevated site with the moor beginning its descent towards Pooley Bridge. The cairn is composed of a variety of stones which stood some 2.1-2.4m (7-8ft) above ground level, with an approximate diameter of 17.3-18.2m (57-60ft). A cist is still clearly visible at the centre of the cairn, the slabs of which are composed of local limestone. The axis of the cist, which was found to contain several entire bones of an adult, is aligned NW-SE on the Kopstone, clearly seen in profile on the mid horizon and may also be orientated along this alignment to the midwinter solstice sunrise or the midsummer solstice sunset.

About 0.5km (0.3m) SW of White Raise is the Cockpit, the largest of the Moor Divock circles. This circle of low stones is set into a bank about 3m (10ft) wide. Many of the stones are now fallen; the tallest of those still upright are just under a metre. The structure of the Cockpit bears some similarity to the embanked circles of the Beacon, Casterton and the Kirk to the S of the county (see the Beacon, Casterton and the Kirk). The Cockpit has been located, together with White Raise, in an alignment with the three sister peaks of the high Pennines, Cross Fell, Little Dun Fell and Great Dun Fell in the NE, down the middle reach of Ullswater to Raise, the highest summit visible on the skyline to the SW. It is tempting to suggest that the naming of the mound White Raise and the mountain of Raise is evidence of this intent. Did the form of the mound mirror the giant-like mound of the mountain?

From the Cockpit the three Pennine peaks are concealed behind White Raise, which is prominent on the near horizon. It is only on the final approach to the top of the mound that this distinctive landform of the Pennines comes into view. Also from the centre of the circle, the summit of Great Mell Fell aligns centrally to the saddle of Blencathra. The location of the Cockpit's

A group of boulders mid-way between the Kopstone and Moor Divock 4, in the middle distance, align on the summit of Heughscar Hill.

position seems to have been determined by these alignments. There is also a skyline barrow on Great Mell Fell which may be contemporary with the circle and which also forms an alignment with Castlerigg stone circle (see Castlerigg).

The Cockpit stone circle is the most prominent of the monuments on the moor and has a diameter of 25m (82ft) and has the remains of what appears to be a cairn to the E. The survey in the late 19th century mentions the remains of a further three cairns within the circle and earthworks can still be discerned in the western arc and in places overlying the circle. In the absence of any excavation report, it cannot be known if any of these were of a sepulchral nature. The same survey mentions the existence of two stone circles, one inside and one outside what now appears to be a wall or bank, but without excavation this is difficult to verify, [see note 2, Appendix V]

FURTHER READING:

Clare, Tom and Wilkinson, David M., *Moor Divock revisited: some new sites, survey and interpretations*, TCWAAS, Volume VI, 2006

RCHM Westmorland.

Simpson, J, *The Antiquities of Shap in the County of Westmorland*, Arch. J, Volume 18, 1861.

Simpson, J, *Stone Circles near Shap, Westmorland*, PSAS (1st Series), volume 4, 1863.

Spence, J E, *An Early Settlement on Moor Divock*, TCWAAS, Volume 34, 1934.

Taylor, M W, *The Prehistoric Remains on Moordivock, near Ullswater*, TCWAAS (Old Series), Vol. 8, 1886.

27. Shapbeck Stone Circle

GRID REF:
NY 5527 1886.

ELEVATION:
269m (883ft).

MAP:
OS Explorer (1:25000) OL5;
OS Landranger (1:50000) 90.

LOCATION:
Latitude 54.33.786;
Longitude 02.41.595:
3.5km (2.1m) N of Shap.

PARKING:
12km (7.4m) S of Penrith,
0.4km (0.25m) N of Shapbeck
Gate on the A6.

WALKING DISTANCE:
0.8km (0.5m).

TERRAIN:
Cultivated farmland.

DESCRIPTION:
SHAPBECK STONE CIRCLE is located on the SE edge of Knipescar Common, overlooking the valleys of the Leith and the Eden in the far distance. The three high peaks of the Pennines, Cross Fell, Little Dun Fell and Great Dun Fell are central to the distant horizon. This aspect forms the focus of Shapbeck and must have determined the circle's position.

An alignment from the centre of the cairn, through the centre of the circle, to the large stone on the outer edge of the second circle, marks the position of the summer solstice sunrise over this distinctive landform of the high Pennines. The largest stone on the eastern edge of the outer circle aligns with the dramatic Pennine landform of High Cup Nick.

This circle was discovered by the Cumbria and Lancashire Archaeological Unit during the Lake District National Park Survey in 1985 and given the name of Shapbeck stone circle. The approximate location and dimensions of the outer circle would suggest that this is the circle which was originally identified by Rev. Canon Simpson, the vicar of Shap, in 1882.

Although exact locations were not given, one of the tumuli in the group identified as belonging to the Knipescar group of antiquities was found to consist of three concentric circles, the outside circle 19.2m (63ft) in diameter, the second 6.4m (21ft), and the inner circle 2.1m (7ft). After its rediscovery in

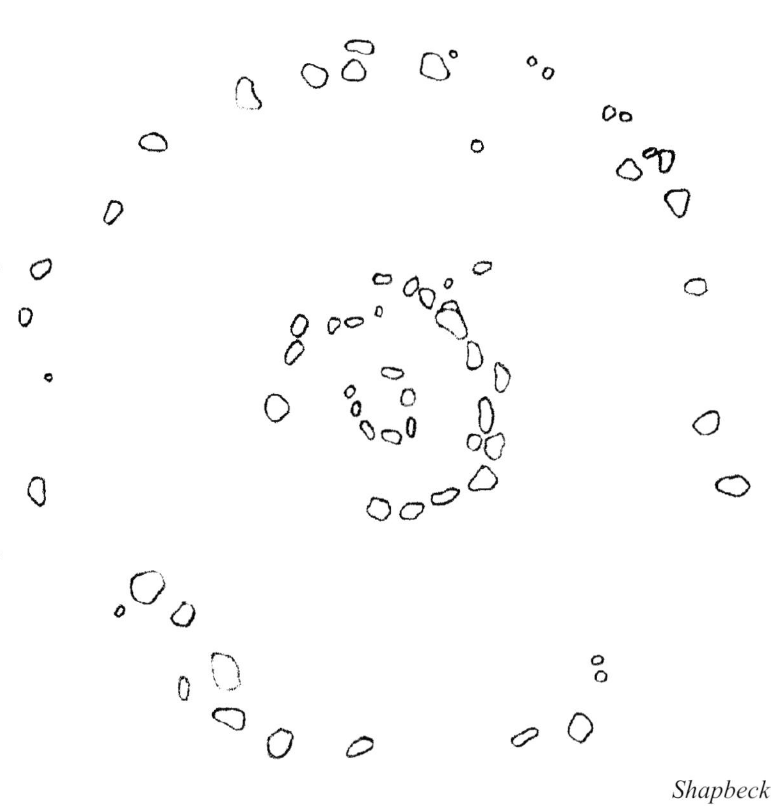

Shapbeck

DETAILED DIRECTIONS:
Just S of Shapbeck Gate, opposite the road for Newby and Morland, follow the public bridleway for Scarside over three stiles routed through agricultural farmland. At the third stile, head WNW uphill to the near horizon; the circle will shortly come into view. During the summer months keep to the field edges. The public bridleway to the Out Scar is within metres of the Shapbeck circle. The circle is on cultivated farmland and is best visited in the lean months of the farming year, between autumn and spring. As summer advances the features of the circle become progressively hidden by agricultural crops.

1985, a subsequent survey of the monument showed that Shapbeck had similar proportions, comprising of three concentric circles; the outer ring had 28 surviving stones with a diameter of 20.5m (67ft), the second ring had eighteen stones and the inner ring seven.

The tallest stones are in the E of the outer circle and stand to a height of 0.9m (3ft) above ground level while the stones of the inner circle are only just visible. Between the outer ring and the second ring, is a cairn of stones in the SW quadrant. This slightly intrudes upon the second ring and possibly indicates that the cairn was secondary to the earlier circle. Some of the stones of the cairn are quite large and possibly come from the circle or from field clearance; some have plough marks on them.

Even today the land is ploughed right up to the margins of the circle. Shapbeck has miraculously survived in an agricultural environment when so many circles have been destroyed, having been deemed an inconvenience to the plough. Simpson also mentions a second circle which was approximately 29m (95.1ft) distant from this one, but doesn't record its direction, size or shape. He does however state that at its centre was found a pavement of cobbles under which was found a deposit of charcoal. Although Shapbeck geographically belongs to the Knipescar group (see The Knipescar Common Stone Circles), the circle also bears close comparison to the Oddendale stone circle group of antiquities (see The Iron Hill Stone Circles) 6km (3.7m) to the S, which also has concentric circles; this would date the circle to the early Bronze Age.

FURTHER READING:

Simpson, J, *The Antiquities of Shap in the County of Westmorland*, Arch. J, Volume 18, 1861.

Simpson, J, Stone Circles near Shap, Westmorland, PSAS (1st Series), Volume 4, 1863.

Turner, V.E. *Shapbeck Stone Circle*, TCWAAS, Volume 86, 1986.

28. Studfold Gate

The circle east of the wall, looking south.

TheNE sector looking south.

DESCRIPTION:

THE CIRCLE is sited on one of the highest points of Dean Moor and commands extensive views of the hills of Dumfries and Galloway to the N, the Lakeland fells to the E, and to the W the coastal plain of the Irish Sea.

The circle is divided in half by a dry stone wall which served as a boundary between the districts of Allerdale and Copeland. On the W side of the circle are the remains of tree stumps amongst the sedge grass, once a dense plantation. At the time of the excavation in the 1920s only one stone was recorded in the plantation although the then owner remembered 'many more stones standing there'.

The better-preserved part of the circle is to the E of the wall, which is pasture. The remains of approximately eight stones are visible, although signs of other possible stones of the circle seem to be buried just beneath the surface; some have been displaced.

The stones are sandstone and have very little visual impact among the sedge grass. The tallest stone to the S is 0.95m (3ft) high and has been incorporated into the wall. Evidence of carved chevrons has been found on one of the stones in the NE sector. The circle, though, is comparatively large and has an oval form measuring approximately 25m (82ft) N-S, with the longer axis at 32m (105ft) E-W.

The most prominent feature of the circle is a mound almost immediately to the west of the wall. It is thought to be a burial cairn, although excavation failed to find any remains. From the centre of the cairn the dramatic, steep saddle between Grisedale Pike, Hopegill Head and Grasmoor is due E. A stone axe was found in the nearby village of Gilgarran. A chronological

GRID REF:
NY 0399 2234.

ELEVATION:
200m (656ft).

MAP:
OS Explorer (1:25000) OL4;
OS Landranger (1:50000) 89.

LOCATION:
Latitude 54.35.229;
Longitude WO 03.29.225:
on the road between
Ullock and Pica, 8km (5miles)
SE of Workington.

PARKING:
Restricted, in vicinity of
Laneside House.

WALKING DISTANCE:
0.25km (0.15m).

TERRAIN:
Pasture, sedge grass and mire.

analysis of the circle's features dates Studfold to c.2500-2000BC, the early Bronze Age.

FURTHER READING:

Mason, J R, and Valentine, H, *Studfold Gate Circle and the Parallel Trenches at Dean*, TCWAAS, Volume 25, 1925.

DETAILED DIRECTIONS:
A gate 100m (350ft) to the E of the former Studfold Public House, now Laneside House and to the N of the road, gives access to a field. Marsh on the lower slopes makes access difficult; make for a conspicuous pile of stone ahead then bear diagonally NE towards the dry stone wall. Follow the wall uphill to the circle approximately 300m (984ft) N of the road. Private Land - access permission required.

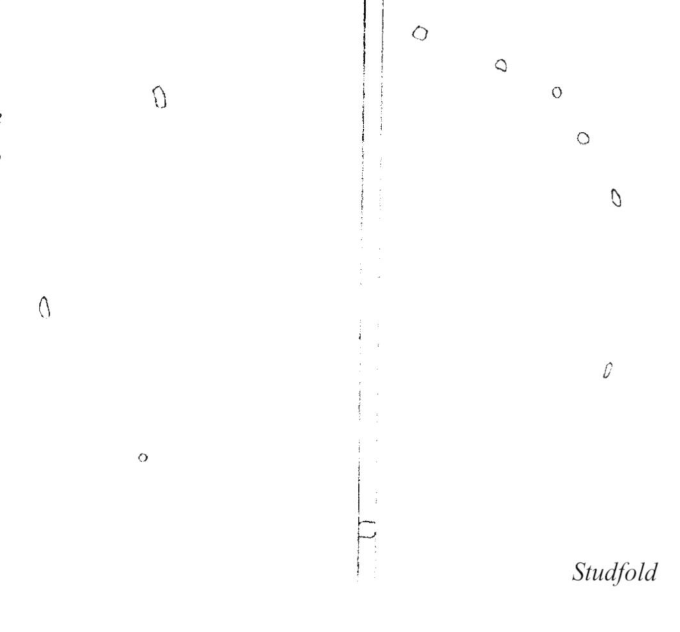

Studfold

The tall southern stone.

29. Swarth Fell Stone Circle

Swarth Fell from the N.

GRID REF:
NY 4565 1919.

ELEVATION:
560m (1837ft).

MAP:
OS Explorer (1:25000) OL5;
OS Landranger (1:50000) 90.

LOCATION:
Latitude N 54.33.903;
Longitude WO 02.50.516:
on Swarth Fell, E of Howtown,
8km (4.9m) SSE
of Pooley Bridge.

PARKING:
In Pooley Bridge or at the top of Roe Head Lane.

WALKING DISTANCE:
8.2km (5.1m) from Pooley Bridge and 6.4km (4m) from Roehead Lane.

TERRAIN:
Bridlepath, high level fell paths, some marsh, rugged steep moor.

DESCRIPTION:

THE HIGH fell wilderness on the approach to the circle has magnificent mountain scenery with the Helvellyn range dominating to the SW, to the WNW Skiddaw and Blencathra, and to the E the high Pennine hills of Cross Fell, Little Dun Fell and Great Dun Fell above the Eden Valley.

The Swarth Fell stone circle has the distinction of being the most isolated in Cumbria, approximately 4km (2.4m) SE of the Cockpit stone circle. It is also one of the most difficult to find and its location seems to be subject to variation even on reputable local maps. The circle is located at the head of the valley of Swarth Beck, with the summit of Loadpot Hill directly S above the near horizon.

From the circle the sun makes its transit across the summit of the hill at midday, and this will almost certainly have influenced the location of the monument. All the stones of the circle are long, slender slabs which have now fallen and lie jumbled in close proximity. Summer grass or an average fall of snow is sufficient to cover and hide the

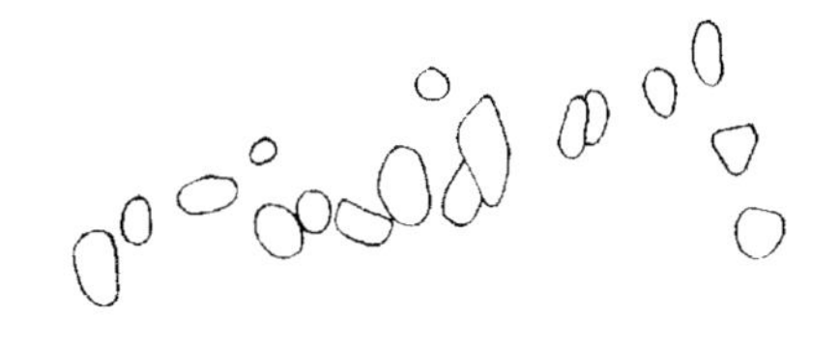

Swarth Fell (after Thom).

DETAILED DIRECTIONS:

Take the lane of Roe Head E of Pooley Bridge on the road to Howtown. Continue along the Public Bridleway for Helton. At a crossroad of tracks marked by a cairn, turn right and continue to the Cockpit stone circle. At the Cockpit take the well-trodden track to the right, and after a short distance, 0.4km (0.25m), the track divides at another cairn. Take the track (which soon becomes a pleasant grassy path) to the left, bearing S around Arthur's Pike and climbing steadily to a boundary stone approximately 2.25km (1.4m) from the last cairn. This is the course of the Roman road of High Street.

On the gradual ascent the broad dome of Loadpot Hill soon comes into view, dominating the southern horizon. After a further 0.8km (0.5m) a second boundary stone is reached. Continue for another 0.8km (0.5m). On nearing the hill a valley opens up to the right, with Swarth Beck flowing north towards Ullswater. The stone circle is just 160m (530ft) below the path and can be seen E of the beck. However, because of its ruinous state, it has very little presence and is difficult to see. If the visibility is good then Blencathra can be seen WNW from here. Alternatively, the circle can also be located by following a bearing N downhill from the vicinity of Loadpot Hill or the Lambert Lad boundary stone, which happens to be almost in alignment between the hill and the circle.

wafer-thin stones, making them difficult to locate.

Many of the stones are absent in the W, yet what appears to be a surviving arc of the circle can be clearly seen, with a diameter of approximately 16m (52ft). The site differs considerably from the survey recorded by Thom in 1955. Closer inspection suggests that this circle is more closely rectangular in form. Whether these differences are a result of disturbances is difficult to ascertain but there is evidence of rapid deterioration since the site was first documented in 1877. A geological survey then described the monument as a ring of standing stones. By 1936 only one stone was left standing.

An estimated 65 stones remain, many of them between 1 and 2m (3.2-6.5ft) in length. The tallest stone of the circle is to the S and has fallen along its flat face, its tapered top possibly once indicating the sun's zenith over Loadpot Hill.

It has been suggested that the stones once resembled the nearby Cockpit in plan, with the inner stones forming an almost continuous wall. The position of both circles also seems to have been determined in relationship to the land forms of nearby fells. The circle, unusually, is located in a hollow enclosed by the valley of Swarth Beck, which offers some protection from the weather in these exposed uplands. This enclosure allows just two open aspects, to the WNW and the N. When descending from the path to the circle the mountains disappear behind the near horizon. Only Blencathra is visible to the WNW from the centre of the circle, seen in a bowl between two knolls in the near horizon.

The main aspect of the circle is to the N where the valley gradually lowers towards Ullswater. The valley of Swarth Beck runs N to S, and the circle seems to have been located halfway along it, between Loadpot and where the valley is lost to view over the precipitous sides of Ullswater. If the circle is contemporary with the nearby Cockpit then it can be tentatively dated to the early Bronze Age.

FURTHER READING:

RCHM Westmorland.

Swarth Fell Stone Circle with Blencathra in the distance.

30. Swinside

Swinside from the N looking towards Knott Hill.

DESCRIPTION:

SWINSIDE IS sometimes known as Sunkenkirk, a name thought to derive from a legend that the Devil pulled down the stones of a church which was being built and sunk them permanently into the ground. It is recorded that the neighbouring people referred to such places as Sunken Kirks. It may well be a memory of the hallowed nature of these places.

The circle compares only to Castlerigg (see Castlerigg) for the visual beauty of its surroundings, but because of its isolation is a quieter site with fewer visitors. It has been described with good reason as being one of the finest stone circles in western Europe.

The circle is enclosed by the higher fells to the W but enjoys a fine open aspect to the E. The circle is sited on ground which appears to have been levelled on the side of a valley, giving the impression of a terrace, with Knott Hill the most distinctive landscape feature to the S. To the W are the fells of Black Combe, which mark the SW limit of the Lakeland range of fells, while away to the NE can be seen the Coniston mountain range. To the SE the valley opens to the Duddon Estuary and the Duddon Sands to the E.

Swinside is an almost complete circle with some 50 remaining stones of porphyritic slate, known locally as 'grey cobbles'. The colour of some of the stones has often been remarked upon and described as 'variously tinted.' The stones are all set close together, sometimes likened to a fence or palisade, spaced about 1.5m (5ft) apart, giving a diameter of 28.6m (94ft). The circle

Swinside from the S.

GRID REF:
SD 1716 8817.

ELEVATION:
207m (679ft).

MAP:
OS Explorer (1:25000) OL6;
OS Landranger (1:50000) 96.

LOCATION:
Latitude N 54.16.948;
Longitude WO 03.16.432:
4km (2.4m) W of
Broughton in Furness.

PARKING:
Restricted parking available in the vicinity of Crag Hall.

WALKING DISTANCE:
1.37km (0.8m).

TERRAIN:
Rough track over fell, pasture.

seems to have clear cardinal trends within its design, with the tallest stone, a long slender pillar measuring 2.3m (7.5ft) due N of the centre and another tall stone almost due S. To the SE is an entrance with two portal stones on either side, 2m (7ft) wide; this is thought to align with the midwinter solstice sunrise from the centre of the circle.

This solstice orientation is also aligned on the Kirk stone circle (see The Kirk) 9.5km distant on Long Moor. Could it be that the name 'Kirk', common to both, is a dim memory of this shared orientation? There is also another solstice orientation suggested for the Long Moor circle. Standing in the centre of the Swinside circle the midsummer solstice sun would rise above the distant summit of the Old Man of Coniston range to the NE. There are several confused references to a circle to the N of Swinside approximately a mile distant, variously described as 'of larger dimensions' and 'being smaller than Sunken Kirk', but its whereabouts is unknown. Swinside shares many of the traits in common with early stone circles like Castlerigg and Long Meg (see Long Meg and her Daughters) and is accordingly dated to the Neolithic period.

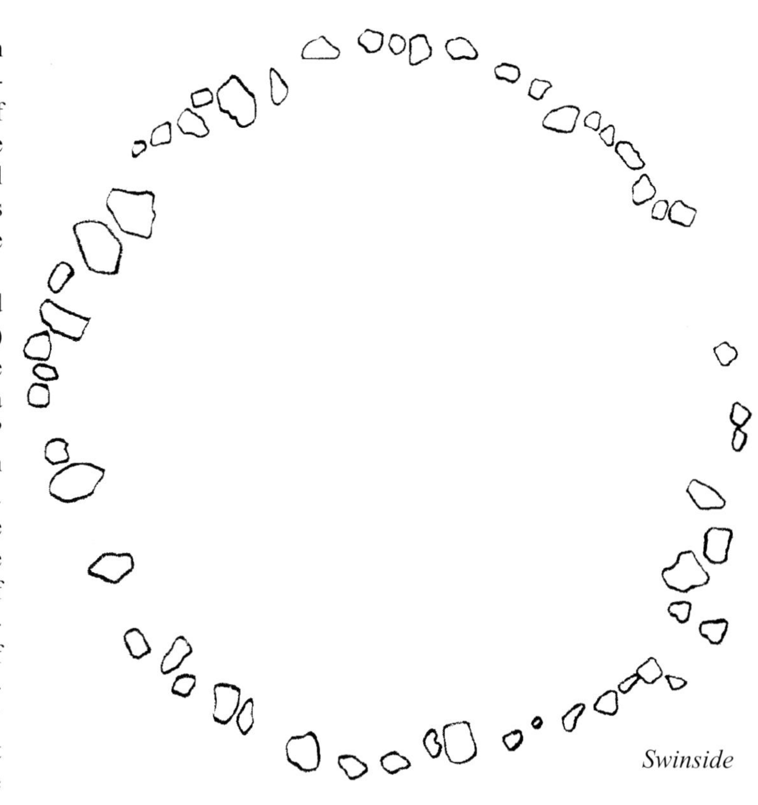
Swinside

FURTHER READING:

Clare, T, *Some Cumbrian Stone Circles in Perspective*, TCWAAS, Volume 75, 1975.
Dymond, C W, *A Group of Cumberland Megaliths*, TCWAAS (Old Series), Volume 5, 1881.
Dymond, C W, *An Exploration at the Megalithic Circle called Sunken Kirk at Swinside in the Parish of Millom, Cumberland,* TCWAAS, Volume 2, 1902.
Hood, S, *Cumbrian Stone Circles, the Calendar and the issue of the Druids*, TCWAAS, Third Series, Volume 4, 2004.
Hood, S. and Wilson, D, *Further Investigations into the Astronomical Alignments at Cumbrian Prehistoric Sites*, TCWAAS, Third Series, Volume 3, 2003.

DETAILED DIRECTIONS:
Follow signs for Broadgate off the A595 and continue through Broadgate towards Crag Hall. Shortly before Crag Hall a public bridleway for Swinside Stone Circle and Thwaites Fell to the left of the lane leads to the circle, which is clearly visible to the right of the track just S of Swinside Farm.

GLOSSARY

Alignment. An arrangement of monuments – standing stones, stone circles, barrows etc. – placed in a straight line. An alignment may include natural landforms but the alignment is more correctly described as orientated to the landform.

Archaeoastronomy. The study of practices and beliefs concerning astronomy in ancient civilisations; the subject is also known as astro-archaeology.

Avenue. A corridor lined with rows of standing stones or an earthen bank and ditch on either side, connecting locations within the same monumental complex, allowing passage from one location to another and thought to be of a processional and ritual nature.

Axis. The principle line central to the symmetry of a monument's construction.

Azimuth. The angular distance in degrees along the horizon measured clockwise from true North.

Barrow. See Cairn.

Beltane. The ancient Celtic festival of May Day, which marked the beginning of summer and was one of the divisions of the ancient solar calendar.

Bronze Age. The period between the Stone and Iron Ages in Western Europe, from approximately 2200 to 500BC, in which metalworking was in bronze.

Cairn. Also referred to as a barrow, mound or tumulus, a cairn can be long or circular in shape and is usually constructed of small stones erected over a burial.

Cairn circle. A kerb of larger stones which surrounded the base of a cairn, and which helped to contain the smaller stones covering the burial (see Introduction).

Candlemas. The Feast of the Purification of the Virgin Mary and the presentation of Christ in the Temple on 2 February. Candlemas falls upon a Scottish Quarter Day, which corresponds with one of the eight divisions of the solar calendar, falling between the solstices and the equinoxes. It is thought to be a Christianised solar festival which formerly marked the end of the first half of winter.

Cap-stone. The covering stone of a burial chamber or cist.

Cardinal Point. The four main points of the compass marking the directions of north, east, south and west (N, S, E and W).

Cinerary urn. A vessel used as a receptacle for the ashes of the dead after cremation.

Cist. A box-shaped burial chamber made of dry stone and covered by a cap-stone, often found beneath a barrow, mound or tumulus.

Concentric stone circle. A stone circle consisting of multiple circles, most commonly two or three, around a common centre (see Introduction).

Cup and ring. Cup and cup and ring carvings are the most prominent amongst the many motifs of megalithic rock art. A cup is a small circular hollow and a cup and ring is a cup mark surrounded by one or more circular rings. The significance of rock art is a mystery but it is thought to be symbolic.

Cursus. A Neolithic structure consisting of parallel banks with internal ditches, resembling an avenue or a path and usually found in association with other monuments such as barrows and stone circles. Thought to be possible processional routes with a ceremonial function.

Druid. A pre-Christian priest of Gaul, Britain or Ireland.

Ellipse/Elliptical. A deviation from a true circle, shaped like a flattened circle. Some stone circles are not truly circular and are best described as elliptical in shape (see Introduction).

Elysium. In Greek myth, a heavenly place where the blessed dwell after death.

Embanked stone circle. A circle of standing stones surrounded by a bank or forming the inner kerb of the bank (see Introduction).

Enclosure. A prehistoric earthwork – an area of land, enclosed either by banks or ditches or a combination of both, often combined with an arrangement of entrances or causeways giving access.

Equinox. The equinox is when the daytime is of equal length as the night; this occurs halfway between the summer and winter solstices. The sun rises in the E and sets directly opposite in the W. This happens twice a year, on the 21 March (the vernal equinox) and on the 23 September (the autumnal equinox).

Erratic. A rock which is different in composition from those of the surrounding landscape, having been transported some distance by glaciation.

Flattened stone circle. Not all stone circles are truly circular and surveys by Alexander Thom identified four main categories of shape; the true circle, the flattened circle, the ellipse and the egg. There are two types of flattened circle which vary in their geometric construction (see Introduction).

Foundation sacrifice. A ritual killing thought to propitiate divine wellbeing and often discovered placed beneath the foundation of the stones of a circle.

Gnomon. The stationary arm of a sundial which casts a shadow. They are more commonly used to tell the time of day, but gnomons can also be used to record the passage of the seasons.

Henge. A Neolithic or Bronze Age enclosure surrounded by an inner ditch and earthen bank with one or more entrances.

Imbolc. A pagan spring festival also known as Imbolg, which shares the same date as Candlemas (1st February) and thought to share the same origin in the ancient solar calendar (see Candlemas).

Kerb-cairn. A cairn in which the smaller stones covering the burial are retained by a kerb of the larger stones around the base. (see Cairn circle).

Kirk. A Scottish word for church, but often found in association with stone circles and other prehistoric earthworks. Very likely reflecting folk traditions in regard to the sacred purpose of these ritual monuments.

Lozenge. An oblique-angled parrallelogram having 4 equal sides, a design which is frequently found decorating megaliths and often incorporated into prehistoric monuments.

Lughnasa. Also known as Lughnasadh and Lammas; it which marked the pagan harvest festival on 1st August and was also a quarter day of the ancient solar calendar.

Megalithic. From the Greek, mega = large, lith = stone. Descriptive of the monuments of the Neolithic and Bronze Ages with their characteristic use of large stones.

Meridian. The solar meridian is when the sun reaches its zenith, its highest point in the sky at midday when it is directly S. An awareness of the meridian is found in many monuments which incorporate a N-S orientation within their design.

Mesolithic. The period of time between the Palaeolithic and the Neolithic, covering the period 12,000 to 3,000BC, characterized by the use of small flint tools.

Mound. See Cairn.

Necropolis. From the Greek, necro = dead; polis = city; city of the dead, a burial sight or cemetery.

Neolithic. The New Stone Age, covering the period 4500 to 2200BC in Europe and characterized by the use of polished stone, flint tools and weapons and the construction of megalithic monuments.

Orientation. The position in relation to the points of the compass indicating direction. A certain feature or the axis of a monument often has an orientation.

Other-world. A spirit world, an after life abode of the dead often located in the west, the region of the setting sun. Natural geographic features such as mountains and islands are often identified as Other-world locations and traditions have attributed many ancient monuments as entrances and touchstones to the Other-world.

Psycho-historic. The historical development of the mind and mental processes.

Rock art. The term given to the many motifs which are carved upon stones and are found on earth fast and outcrop rocks, and also adorning monuments such as standing stones, stone circles and cairns (see Cup and ring).

Romanticism. The philosophy of the Romantic movement in art, literature and music in the late 18th and early 19th centuries.

Rough-out. The first stage in the development of a stone axe. A piece of stone which has been shaped to the approximate form of an axe head.

Saddle. Descriptive term given to a landform between two peaks which resembles a saddle, Blencathra in the Lake District is a classic example. It is also a Col, the lowest point in a ridge between two peaks, often the place of a pass from one valley to another.

Samhain. Samhain fell on 1st November; Halloween is a survival of this pagan festival, which marked the beginning of winter, and was regarded as a time when the supernatural world was felt to be close.

Sepulchural. Relating to the sepulchre and suggestive of a burial place; tomb-like.

Shadow path. The shadow of a stone cast by the rising or setting sun. Such phenomena have often been shown to possess some astronomical, directional and constructional significance.

Solstice. From the Latin, sol = sun, stice = stand; the sun's standstill, when the sun reaches its extreme positions along the horizon at midsummer and midwinter. At such times there is no noticeable difference in the movement of the rising and setting positions of the sun for about 3-4 days.

Spiral. One of the more frequently occurring symbols found in rock art, there are two types of spiral, the clockwise spiral and the anti-clockwise spiral (see rock art and cup and ring).

Tumulus. See Cairn.

BIBLIOGRAPHY

Beckensall, S, *Prehistoric Rock Art in Cumbria* (Stroud, Tempus Publishing, 2002)

Bland, J S, c. 1860, *The Vale of Lyvennett,* Parker, F H M (ed), (Titus Wilson, 1910)

Bicknell, Peter, *Beauty, Horror and Immensity: Picturesque Landscape in Britain,1750-1850*, (Cambridge, Cambridge University Press, 1981)

Bradley, R, *An Archaeology of Natural Places* (London, Routledge, 2000)

Bradley, R. & Edmonds, M, *Interpreting the Axe Trade: Production and Exchange in Neolithic Britain* (Cambridge, Cambridge University Press, 2005)

Burl, A, *From Carnac to Callanish: the Prehistoric Stone Rows and Avenues of Britain, Ireland and Brittany* (London: Yale University Press, 1993)

Burl, A, *Great Stone Circles* (London: Yale University Press, 1999)

Burl, A, *The Stone Circles of Britain, Ireland and Brittany* (London, Yale University Press, 2000)

Burl, A, '"Without sharp north…" Alexander Thom and the Great Stone Circles of Cumbria', in C.L.N Ruggles (ed) *Records in Stone: Papers in Memory of Alexander Thom* (Cambridge: Cambridge University Press, 1988)

Clare, T, *Archaeological Sites of the Lake District* (Ashbourne: Moorland Publishing, 1981)

Clare, T, *Prehistoric Monuments of the Lake District* (Tempus, 2007)

Cowan, T, 'Megalithic Compound Ring Geometry', in C.L.N. Ruggles (ed) *Record in Stone: Papers in Memory of Alexander Thom* (Cambridge: Cambridge University Press, 1988)

Curtis, R, 'The Geometry of some Megalithic Rings', in C.L.N. Ruggles (ed) *Records in Stone: Papers in Memory of Alexander Thom* (Cambridge: Cambridge University Press, 1988)

Edmonds, M, *The Langdales: Landscape and Prehistory in a Lakeland Valley* (Stroud: Tempus, 2004)

Harris, R, *Walks in Ancient Lakeland* (Wilmslow: Sigma Leisure, 2001)

Heggie, C. D, *Megalithic Science. Ancient Mathematics and Astronomy in Northwest Europe* (London: Thames and Hudson, 1981)

Hodgson, Rev, *A topographical and historical description of the County of Westmorland* (London, 1811)

Hutchinson, W, *The History of the County of Cumberland* (Carlisle: Jollie, 1794)

Lefebure, M, *The Illustrated Lake Poets* (Leicester: Windward, 1987)

MacFarlane, R, *Mountains of the Mind: a History of a Fascination* (London: Granta, 2003)

Machell, T, c. 1690 Manuscript *History of Westmorland*, six volumes in Carlisle Record Office.

Michell, J, *Megalithomania* (London: Thames and Hudson, 1982)

Nicolson, J & Burn, R, *The History and Antiquities of the Counties of Westmorland and Cumberland* (London: Strachan, 1777)

Parker, C.A and Collingwood, W.G, *The Gosforth District: Its Antiquities and Places of Interest* (Kendal: Titus Wilson, 1926)

Pennant, T, *A Tour in Scotland and voyage to the Hebridges*, (Warrington, 1772)

Pennant, T, *A Tour in Scotland*, Third ed. (Warrington: Eyres, 1774)

Royal Commission for Historical Monuments (London: Stationery Office, 1936)
Ruggles, C, *Astronomy in Prehistoric Britain and Ireland* (Yale University Press, 1999)
Simpson. J.Y, *Archaic Sculpturings of Cups and Circles* (Edinburgh: Edmonton and Douglas, 1867)
Thom, A, *Megalithic Sites in Britain* (Oxford: Oxford University Press, 1967)
Thom, A, *Megalithic Lunar Observatories* (Oxford: Oxford University Press, 1973)
Thom, A & Thom, A.S, *Megalithic Remains in Britain and Brittany* (Oxford: Oxford University Press, 1978)
Tilley, C, *A Phenomenology of Landscape: Places, Paths and Monuments* (Oxford: Berg, 1994)
Waterhouse, J, *The Stone Circles of Cumbria* (Chichester: Phillimore, 1985)
Watson, A. & Bradley, R, 'On the Edge of England: Cumbria as a Neolithic Region' in G. Barclay and K. Brophy (eds) *Regional Diversity in the Neolithic of Britain and Ireland* (Oxford: Oxbow, in press)
Watson, A. 'Making Space for Monuments: Notes on the Representation of Experience' in Elizabeth DeMarrais, Chris Gosden & Colin Renfrew (eds) *Substance, Memory, Display: Archaeology and Art* (McDonald Institute Monographs) (Cambridge: McDonald Institute for Archaeological Research, 2004a)
Watson, A, 'Monuments that made the World: Performing the Henge', in R. Cleal and J. Pollard (eds) *Monuments and Material Culture: Papers in Honour of an Avebury Archaeologist, Isobel Smith* (East Knoyle: Hobnob Press, 2004b)
Watson, A, 'Fluid Horizons', in Vicki Cummings and Chris Fowler (eds) *The Neolithic of the Irish Sea* (Oxford: Oxbow, 2004c)
Whellan, W, *The History and Topography of the Counties of Cumberland and Westmorland* (Pontefract: Whellan, 1860)
Wordsworth, W, Poem XLIII. 'The Monument commonly called Long Meg and her Daughters, Near the River Eden', 1822

BIBLIOGRAPHICAL NOTE:

Within the Bibliograpy are listed all the major works of reference. In addition to these, each individual site entry within the guide contains further references to reports of a more specific and specialized nature. These are usually the local archaeological reports and often the original excavation reports, where they exist. It is hoped that these will be of interest to the visitor who wishes to further an understanding of any particular site.

BIBLIOGRAPHICAL ABBREVIATIONS:

Arch	Archaeologia
Arch. J	Archaeological Journal
CW 1, 2 and 3	The Cumberland and Westmorland Antiquarian and Archaeological Society, Old, New and Third Series
PSAL	Proceedings of the Society of Antiquaries of London
PSAS	Proceedings of the Society of Antiquaries of Scotland
RCHM Westmorland	Royal Commission on Historical Monuments, England, An Inventory of the Historical Monuments in Westmorland (1936)
TCWAAS	Transactions of the Cumberland & Westmorland Antiquarian & Archaeological Society.

Appendix I

Gazetteer of Cumbrian Stone Circles

Annaside: SD 099 853: documented: a stone circle 1 km (0.6m) NW of Gutterby, now destroyed was reported in the 18th and 19th centuries. One surviving stone of a circle of twelve with a possible diameter of 18m (59ft) which may have had a central mound.

Appleby Hill: SD 289 743: This oval cairn 12.5m (41ft) x 10m (32.8ft) with an axis ESE-WNW on Appleby Hill is NE of the Druid Circle on Birkrigg Common. The eastern sector covered a small stone circle 3.6m (11.8ft) x 3.9m (12.7ft), the stones of which leaned inward. Within the circle were found dark deposits of earth which contained possible shards of prehistoric pottery. Also within the cairn was found a skeleton with an awl and near the centre some pieces of a skull.

Ash House: SD 193 873: documented: This stone circle once located on a hillside near Ash House overlooked the Duddon Estuary. The circle is thought to be the one described in the early 19th century as being not far from Swinside. The stones were described as being small and only 22 surviving appearing above the surface. If this is the circle referred to then only two surviving stones now remain, these are 30 m (98.4ft) apart, suggesting a circle with a diameter of approximately 38m (124.6ft). The two surviving stones are ina NE-SW alignment suggesting a possible astronomical orientation to either the summer solstice sunrise or the midwinter sunset.

Banniside: see Guide.

The Beacon: see Guide.

Birkrigg Common – the Druid Circle: see Guide.

Blakeley Raise: see Guide.

Bleaberry Haws: see Guide.

Brackenber and the Shap Avenue: see Guide – **Kemp Howe and the Shap Avenue.**

Brat's Hill: see Guide – **The Burnmoor Circles.**

Broadfield: NY 43 45: documented: exact location unknown but approximately 11km (6.8m) SSE of Carlisle, 1.5km (0.9m) W of Broadfield House and E of Roe Beck. It was described in the late 18th century as consisting of six large stones arranged in three pairs around a low circular mound 19.2m (62.9ft) in diameter. Within the area of the mound were found three large cists which seem to suggest that the monument may have been a cairn circle. It has also been reported that there were other stones nearby in whic it was possible to detect an avenue. No visible remains.

Broomrigg A: see Guide – **Broomrigg.**

Broomrigg B: see Guide – **Broomrigg.**

Broomrigg C: see Guide – **Broomrigg.**

Broomrigg D: see Guide – **Broomrigg.**

Brougham Hall: documented: exact location unknown; somewhere on the northern bank of the River Eamont opposite Mayburgh Henge. A cairn circle 'composed of round stones, and surrounded with large grit stones of different sizes, some a yard square, which all together form a circle sixty feet in diameter.' A site fitting this description is illustrated by William Stukeley in his drawing of Mayburgh Henge in 1725. No visible remains.

Casterton: see Guide.

Castlehowe Scar: see Guide – the **Iron Hill Circles.**

Castlerigg: see Guide.

Castlerigg W: documented: exact location unknown; in an adjoining field, W-SW of Castlerigg. No visible remains.

Chapel Flat: NY 37 50: documented: exact location unknown but near the village of Dalston, 7km (4.3m) SW of Carlisle. Described in the 18th century as a circle of stones with an approximate diameter of 27m (88ft). Four large stones lay E of the centre, which may have been the remains of a cist. No visible remains.

The Cockpit: see Guide – **The Moor Divock Stone Circles.**

Elva Plain: see Guide.

Gamelands: see Guide.

Gaythorne Plain: NY 646 111: documented: This site possibly described in the 19th century as a group of concentric circles and avenue is now quite confused. The site consists of a stoney earthwork approximately 16m (52.4ft) in diameter with a possible entrance to the N and a smaller grouping of stones at the centre. There is a bank of stones to the N which is the probably avenue altough another grouping of stones to the E has also been interpreted as this feature.

Gaythorne Plain 2: NY 648 119: documented: Two possible cairn circles are located on slopes either side of a shallow valley. The one in the W had been subject to excavation in the late 19th century and the bones of an adult were found near the surface at the centre of the mound, three stones appeared to form a kerb to the S of the mound. During the same period the one in the E also yielded the remains of two bodies near the centre, this cairn had a circle of stones around the base. The stones can still be seen although the stones from the eastern site seem to have been displaced because they are at some distance from the mound.

Gaythorne Hall: NY 649 133: documented: N of the previous sites a cairn circle was excavated behind Gaythorne Hall in the late 19th century. The cairn was reported to have a 'circle of stones' around the base. The remains of three bodies were found within the cairn, one burnt body in the centre and the bones of two bodies in the SE sector.

Glassonby: see Guide.

Grasmere: NY 34 08: documented: exact location unknown but near where the road from Keswick meets the road to Grasmere. Described in the early 19th century as consisting of several large stones, circular in form, many of which had been moved and possibly broken up for roads. No visible remains.

Gretigate A: see Guide – **The Gretigate Circles.**

Gretigate B: see Guide – **The Gretigate Circles.**

Gretigate C: see Guide – **The Gretigate Circles.**

Grey Croft: see Guide.

Grey Yauds: NY 545 487: documented: located on King Harry Moor, 2.75km (1.7m) NNE of Ainstable and has been described as being located in a natural pass between the Eden and the Pennines. It is thought to be one of the large early circles consisting of 88 large stones of granite with a diameter of 47.5m (156ft). The circle had been destroyed by 1816 and the stones used for walls during enclosure. Many large stones possibly belonging to the circle can be seen in the base of the wall to the W. The only remaining stone is an outlier 5m (16ft) to the NE, which was taller than the other stones none of which were more than 1.2m (3.9ft) in height. Sources differ concerning the exact location of the outlier - placing it either in the NE or NW. The existence of a more distant outlier together with two mounds has also been reported about 2,000ft (608m) to the SE.

Gunnerkeld: see Guide.

Gutterby: SD 106 848: documented: This site has also been known as Kirkstones and consisted of 30 stones forming part of two concentric circles. The circle no longer exists but a recent topographical survey suggests that the outer circle was around 20-28m (65.6-91.8ft) in diameter with the inner one, which was reported as being near complete being some 14m. There was also a large cairn 182.8m (600ft) to the S of the circle which had a diameter of 13.5m (44.2ft) 'surrounded with large stones at the base' but this also no longer survives.

Hackthorpe Stone Circle: NY 548 231: documented: This burial mound was destroyed in the 19th century but is well documented. Beneath it was a stone circle with a diameter of 20m (65.6ft). Several cremations were found within the circle in the NW and SE quadrants and at the centre. These cremations were placed in pits which were covered with a dome of cobbles, an arrangement which it is suggested is indicative of them being placed in an open circle prior to the construction of the mound.

Haberwain Stone Circle: NY 59 14: documented: In the vicinity of Iron Hill N and Iron Hill S, between Harberwain Rigg and Harberwain Plantation, was a circle of stones 7.3m (24ft) in diameter 'within which had been a mound'.

Hardendale Fell: NY 5732 1240: This group of stones was first reported in a survey for a gas pipeline and only gets its first mention in archaeological literature recently (Clare, 2007). Some of the stones are still upright and do appear to form a circle.

Harkeld Stone Circle: NY 58 15: documented: The site of this circle is mentioned by 19th century antiquarians but the place cannot now be identified. It is thought that this circle may be the one at Castlehow Scar. The place of Harkeld in shown on Hodgson's 1828 map of Westmorland showing a small area of unenclosed common and the circle of Castlehowe Scar is to the E of this area. The description of theHarkeld circle being '... formed by ten stones and is 5.4m (18ft) in diameter' bears a close comparison to Castlehowe Scar. It is also mentioned that while digging at the Harkeld circle a 'stratum of charred bones' were found.

Hall Foss: SD 112 857: documented: exact location unknown but approximately E of the A595, 2.5km

(1.5m) S of Bootle and 1km (0.6m) N of Stangrah farm. Described as eight large stones with a diameter of 23m (25yds). It was destroyed in the late 18th to early 19th centuries. No visible remains.

Hird Wood: see Guide.

Iron Hill N: see Guide – **The Iron Hill Circles.**

Iron Hill S: see Guide – **The Iron Hill Circles.**

Kemp Howe and the Shap Avenue: see Guide.

King Arthur's Round Table: see Guide – **Mayburgh Henge and King Arthur's Round Table.**

The Kirk: see Guide.

Kirkstones: SD 106 843: documented: located 3.75km (2.3m) NW of Silecroft and 4km (2.4m) S of Bootle on Green Moor Farm 270m (890ft) SE of Gutterby and 1.5km (0.9m) SSW of Hall Foss. Described as two concentric circles 'similar in position to those of Stonehenge'. The diameters of the circles have not been recorded but there were thirty stones extant. No visible remains.

Knipescar Common Stone Circle: see Guide.

The Kopstone Circle: see Guide – **The Moor Divock Stone Circles.**

Lacra A: see Guide – **The Lacra Circles.**

Lacra B: see Guide – **The Lacra Circles.**

Lacra C: see Guide – **The Lacra Circles.**

Lacra D: see Guide – **The Lacra Circles.**

Lamplugh: documented: NY 065 177: located 3km (1.8m) E of Frizington, 1km (0.6m) SW of Rowrah and 1km (0.6m) N of Stockhow Hall. Described in 1842, when only the northern section of the circle existed, as consisting of six stones 'nearly 4ft above the ground'. The other stones of the circle had been destroyed and removed to make walls a few years previously. It was estimated that the diameter would have been approximately '100 paces' making this a very impressive circle. No visible remains.

Le Wheles: documented: NX 989 180: located 1km (0.6m) E of the centre of Whitehaven, where the St Bees Register records that a building called 'Standing Stones' was the site of Le Wheles. It is thought to be the circle referred to by R. G. Collingwood as 'Corkickle', which was destroyed in 1628. No visible remains.

Leacet Hill: see Guide.

Levens Park: 50 86: documented: This site was most probably a cairn circle and was the subject of excavation prior to the construction of a dual carriageway. The central cairn was surrounded by a circular stone kerb approximately 25m (82ft) in diameter. There were two similar sized gaps in the outer kerb ENE and WSW, reminiscent of similarities in the stone circles of Swinside and Gamelands.

Little Asby Common: NY 680 083: This small circle of stones is located on the spur of a ridge overlooking Sunbiggin Tarn. There are more stones at the centre and the arrangement it has been suggested could be indicative of a cist. There seems to be an alignment SE from the circle to a nearby mound approximately 20m

(65.6ft) distant; the alignment continues to an outlier a further 10m (32.8ft) from the mound. The alignment of these monuments seems to be located cenral to the spur of this ridge.

Little Meg (The Maughanby Stone Circle): see Guide.

Long Meg and her Daughters: see Guide.

Long Meg SW: see Guide – **Long Meg and her Daughters.**

Low Longrigg SW: see Guide – **The Burnmoor Circles.**

Low Longrigg NE: see Guide – **The Burnmoor Circles.**

Oddendale: see Guide – **The Iron Hill Circles.**

Mayburgh Henge: see Guide – **Mayburgh Henge and King Arthur's Round Table.**

Moor Divock 4: see Guide – **The Moor Divock Stone Circles.**

Moor Divock 5: see Guide – **The Moor Divock Stone Circles.**

Motherby: documented: NY 419 282: located 1km (0.6m) W of the village Motherby, N of the A66 between Keswick and Penrith. The circle was approximately 15.5m (50.8ft) in diameter. A circular bank protruding 'platform-like' from a hillside has been identified as the probable site of the circle and is just visible from the A66 - it has been suggested that the site is reminiscent of a cairn circle. W. G. Collingwood, writing in 1923, thought that a stone survived from this circle, and there is a standing stone nearby but there is an extensive field of glacial material adjacent to the site. However there are several large stones in the vicinity and others can be seen in the bases of ruined walls. It was destroyed in the first half of the 19th century.

Oddendale Cairn Circle: NY 590 135: documented: Discovered by Clare as a research student in the mid-1960s. He excavated it prior to its destruction. Beneath the cairn was found 'two concentric circles of posts.' At some stage the posts had been removed and the pits 'capped with boulders so as to remain visible.' The cairn was built to a height of 0.3m with an approximate diameter of 20m.

Ormstead Hill: NY 50 27: documented: See Redhills below.

Penhurrock: NY 628 104: documented: This site has also been referred to as Robin Hood's Grave. Described as a cairn 18.2m (60ft) in diameter with an internal circle of stones 10m (33ft) in diameter, surrounding a central cist. This is now a confused site due to quarrying which consists mostly of Shap granite boulders. Some of the boulders do give the appearance of being grouped in arcs and the base of the mound seems to have been preserved in places. The quarrying of the cairn led to the discovery of an 'abundance of decayed human bones.'

Potter Fell: documented: SD 503 988: located 6.5km (4m) N of Kendal on Potter Fell. The site was described in 1960 as a stone circle consisting of some 20 low stones of approximately 20m (66ft) in diameter. The circle is located on a natural ridge and the stones could be the kerb of a mound. Although looking like an early Bronze Age circle, its authenticity has been doubted and it is thought to have been a cockpit.

Rawthey Bridge: SD 71 98: documented: exact location unknown but thought to have been alongside the road between Kirkby Stephen and Sedbergh, near Rawthey Bridge. Described briefly as a Druidic circle of large stones. No visible remains.

Redhills: NY 501 277: documented: Redhills is the place where what has been described as 'The most remarkable cup-marked stone discovered...' which was found in 1881 where it had been used as a cist cover. No mention is made of a mound or a cairn but Dr Taylor who discovered the stone does mention other possible sites in the locality. Not far to the S, approximately 274.3m (900ft) was a round cairn on the slope of a hill and also 'near the top of a hill, not far distant, what might be the remains of a small sepulchral circle, with some stones partially buried.' This latter site may be the circle which was reported to be located on Ormstead Hill.

Ringlen Stones, Egremont: NX 995 107: documented: exact location unknown but 1.6km (0.99m) W of Egremont. Very little is known of the monument other than it consisted of ten large stones '60 paces' in diameter. No visible remains.

Sandford Stone Circle: NY 71 17: documented: Its exact location is unknown but has been described as being alongside the Roman Way, now the A66. The only known reference to this large stone circle is a note and drawing by Thomas Machell in an unpublished manuscript c1690. The circle is described as consisting of an embankment of earth and stone and upon this 'are pitched several great stones almost at equal distances, and some again of a lesser size are placed betwixt them... with the whole diameter about 50 paces...' No visible remains.

Sewborrens: NY 485 302: documented: Located at a farm SE of Newton Reigny there is recorded to have been the 'remnants of a stone sepulchral ring at Sewborrns' and a buried 'stone circle' at 'the Riggs.' The exact locations are unknown. No visible remains.

Shapbeck Stone Circle: see Guide.

Solden Hill: NY 43 45: documented: A site near to Broadfield (see Broadfield) has been described as a mound some 13m (42.6ft) in diameter with a circle of granite stones on top. Several cists were found within the mound containing a variety of human bones. No visible remains.

Studfold Gate: see Guide.

Summerhouse Hill Stone Circle: SD 501 742: documented: located on Summerhouse Hill 3.5km (2.1m) N of Carnforth and just W of Yealand Conyers. The circle consists of six large limestone megaliths, four of which suggest the remains of a large circle 460ft (140m) in diameter. There are outliers 100m (335ft) to the SSE and 100m (335ft) to the W of the centre. A summerhouse was erected within the circle in the mid 18th century and the missing stones are thought to have been broken up to build the plinth.

Swarth Fell: see Guide.

Swinside: see Guide.

Threaplands: NY 592 174: documented: The existence of this circle has not been recognised until recently. It was first mentioned in 1910 by Bland and more recently by Clare (2007). The latter recognises that although the circle may be the result of field clearance, its location bears some characteristics with other stone circles. Like these the circle is located on the break of a slope at the southern end of a ridge 'where it merges with the hillside' and there is also a possible outlier which is directly S of the circle. The stones are seven in number as was recorded by Bland who also found the butt end of a stone axe nearby. The mound on nearby Winrigg's Hill due W across the valley may also have once been visible from the circle.

White Hag: see Guide – **The Iron Hill Circles.**

White Moss SW: see Guide – **The Burnmoor Circles.**

White Moss NE: see Guide – **The Burnmoor Circles.**

White Raise: see Guide – **The Moor Divock Stone Circles.**

Wilson Scar: NY 549 182: documented: located S of Knipe Scar 4km (2.4m) NNW of Shap. This circle was well-documented, together with an accurate plan, in 1935, and was excavated in 1952 before quarry workings threatened to encroach upon the site. The circle consisted of 35 prostrate stones with an approximate diameter of 18m (60ft). No visible remains.

Appendix II

List of the Cumbrian Stone Circle Notebooks from the Alexander Thom Archive*

Compiled by Dr Ian Fraser.

Ms 430/09
1952: 1952 Sept. Lakes: Tarnmoor; Sunken Kirk; Burnside; Elver Plain; Castlerigg.

Ms 430/10
1953: Orton.

Ms 430/12
1953: Long Meg; Little Meg; Glen; Lundin Links; Burrow bridge: Devils' Arrows.

Ms 430/19
1955: 1955 Easter. Lakes. High Street; Castle Rigg; Seascale, Boot?; Giants Graves; Lacra; Birkrigg: Wayland Smithy.

Ms 430/30
1959, 1960: 1959, Burnmoor; Castle Rigg: 1960, Wales; Fowlis Wester; Pitlochry; Dowally.

Ms 430/63
1966: Burnmoor; Ennerdale; Castle Rigg: Escart; Loch Stornoway; Kilberry; Slockvulluin; Sui…?; Duncracaig;….Circle?; Kintraw; Jura: Gigha; Temple Wood; Poltalloch.

*This is a basic listing of the notebooks compiled from the cover and flyleaf information in each volume. In the complete listings there are a total of 99 notebooks which run in almost consecutive order with the notable absence of the years 1940, 1941, 1942, 1949, 1967 and 1978. However, there are four notebooks which are not dated and its likely that some of the absent years belong to these. The Alexander Thom Archive is held in the National Monuments Record of Scotland.

Appendix III

Catalogue of the Cumbrian Stone Circles Surveys from the Alexander Thom Archive*

Compiled by Lesley Ferguson.

The format of the entries is as follows:

1. Name of site.
2. Classification.
3. National Monuments Record of Scotland (NMRS) site number.
4. National grid reference.
5. NMRS reference of the individual drawings within the Drawings Collection of the National Monuments Record of Scotland. The suffixes used indicate whether a drawing is a copy (/c) or that the original is not in NMRS (/co, copy only).
6. Professor Thom's catalogue number.
7. Inscription on drawing.
8. Details of drawing.
9. Scale (as defined by Thom).
10. Medium.
11. Paper size (height x width in mm)
12. Paper type if not drawn on cartridge paper.
13. Date, if written on the drawing.

* The Alexander Thom Archive is held in the National Monuments Record of Scotland.

CUMBERLAND

Blakeley Raise
Stone Circle
NY01SE6
NY0601 1403
DC4531
L1/16
Insc. Blakeley Moss
Annotated plan of stone circle with outline sketch of Screel Hill, Kirkcudbright
1 in: 8ft
Blue ink and pencil
555mm x 385mm

Blakeley Raise
(see above)
DC4772
L1/16
Insc. Blakeley Moss
Plan of stone circle with sketch of Screel Hill, Kirkcudbright
1/4 in: 2ft
Black ink
369mm x 288mm
Plastic film

Blakeley Raise
(see above)
DC4895
L1/16
Insc. Blakeley Moss
Horizon profile of Screel Hill, Kirkcudbright

No scale
Black ink
254mm x 202mm
Plastic film

Brats Hill
Stone circle
NY 10SE 1
NY 173023
DC4521
L1/6
Plan of stone circle
1/8 in: 1ft
Pencil
555mm x 364mm
Tracing paper

Brats Hill
(see above)
DC4522
L1/6
Insc. Burnmoor (E)
Plan of stone circle
1/8 in: 1 ft
Black ink and pencil
558mm x 381mm
1955

Brats Hill
(see above)
DC4523
L1/6
Insc. Burnmoor Circle E
Annotated plan of stone circle
1/8 in: 1 ft
Blue ink and pencil
558mm x 380mm
1959

Brats Hill
(see above)
DC4515
L1/6
Insc. Burnmoor Circles
Plan showing the positions of the stone circles to each other with chart showing circle centres as measured in 1966
3/4 in: 100ft
Pencil
557mm x 317mm

Brats Hill
(see above)
DC4520
L1/6
Insc. Burnmoor, 1st survey
Annotated plan showing position of stone circle in relation to circles C and D.
1 in: 100ft
Pencil
559mm x 326mm

Castle Rigg
Stone Circle
NY22SE 1
NY29142363
DC4505
L1/1
Insc. Castle Rigg
Annotated plan of stone circle
1/8 in: 1 ft
Black ink and pencil
559 mm x 385 mm

Castle Rigg
(see above)
DC4506
L1/1
Plan of stone circle showing flattened
circle shape
No scale
Red and green ink
553 mm x 372 mm
Tracing paper

Castle Rigg
(see above)
DC4507
L1/1
Plan of stone circle. Annotated '1st survey. Drawn too large by 1 ft on
diam[eter)'.
No scale
Black ink and pencil
458 x 372 mm
Linen backed tracing paper

Castle Rigg
(see above)
DC4508
L1/1
Insc. Castle Rigg, 1959 survey
Plan of stone circle
1/8 in: 1 ft
Blue ink and pencil
558 mm x 381 mm

Castle Rigg
(see above)
DC4776
L1/1
Insc. Castle Rigg
Drawing illustrating the stones and horizon as seen from the centre of the circle and showing the rising and setting positions of various celestial bodies
No scale
Black, red and green ink
845 mm x 155 mm

Elva Plain
Stone Circle
NY13SE 4
NY 177 317
DC4509
L1/2
Insc. Elver Plain, Setmurthy
Plan of stone circle
1/8 in: 1 ft
Black ink and pencil
562 mm x 382 mm

Giant's Grave
Standing Stones
SD18SW 12
SD136 803
DC4528
L1/11
Insc. Giant's Graves
Plan of standing stones
1/4 in: 1 ft
Black and pencil
557 mm x 295 mm

Giant's Grave
(see above)
DC4855/co
L1/11
Insc. Giant's Graves
Plan of standing stones with a hillside sketch
1/5 in: 1 ft
Dyeline copy
203 mm x 117 mm

Glassonby
Cairn Circle
NY53NE 2
NY57283935
DC4526
L1/9
Insc. Glassonby
Plan of stone circle
1/8 in: 1 ft
Black ink and pencil
560 mm x 370 mm

Grey Croft
Stone Circle
NY00SW 3
NY03340238

DC4527
L1/10
Insc. Seascale
Plan of stone circle
1/8 in: 1 ft
Black ink and pencil
559 mm x 383 mm

Lacra A
Stone Circle
SD18SE 2
SD15128125
DC4529
L1/12
Insc. Lacra E
Plan of stone circle
1/8 in: 1 ft
Black ink and pencil
558 x 318 mm

Lacra B
Stone Circle
SD18SW 3
SD15008096
DC4529
L1/13
Insc. Lacra S
Plan of stone circle
1/8 in: 1 ft
Black ink and pencil
558 mm x 318 mm

Little Meg
Cairn
NY53NE 14
NY57703748
DC4525
L1/8
Insc. Little Meg
Plan of cairn
1/4 in: 1 ft
Black ink and pencil
559 mm x 374 mm

Long Meg and her Daughters
Stone Circle
NY53NE 5
NY57113721
DC4524
L1/7
Insc. Long Meg and her Daughters
Annotated plan of stone circle
3/8 in: 10 ft
Black ink and pencil
553 mm x 388 mm

Low Longrigg NE
Stone Circle
NY10SE 2
NY172 027
DC4511
L1/4
Insc. Burnmoor A, 1952 Rough Survey
Plan of stone circle with tracing from the 6-in. OS map showing the positions of circles A, B, C, D and E.
1/10 in: 1 ft
Black ink and pencil
558 mm x 381 mm

Low Longrigg NE
(see above)
DC4512
L1/4
Insc. Burnmoor A, Circle A 1959 Survey
Annotated plan of stone circle
1/10 in: 1 ft
Blue ink and pencil
558 x 384 mm
1959

Low Longrigg NE
(see above)
DC4515
L1/6
Insc. Burnmoor Circles
Plan showing the position of the stone circle in relation to

the others with chart showing circle centres as measured in 1966
3/4 in: 100 ft
Pencil
557 mm x 317 mm

Low Longrigg SW
Stone Circle
NY10SE 2
NY172 027
L1/4
Insc. Burnmoor B
Plan of stone circle
1/10 in: 1 ft
Blue ink and pencil
559 mm x 375 mm
1952

Low Longrigg SW
(see above)
DC4514
L1/4
Insc. Burnmoor, Circle B, 1959 Survey
Plan of stone circle
1/10 in: 1 ft
Blue ink and pencil
557 mm x 381 mm
1959

Low Longrigg SW
(see above)
DC4515
L1/4
Insc. Burnmoor Circles
Plan showing the position of the stone circle in relation to the others with chart showing circle centres as measured in 1966
3/4 in: 100 ft
Pencil
557 mm x 317 mm

Studfold
Stone Circle
NY02SW 6
NY040 223
DC4530
L1/14
Insc. Dean Moor
Anotated plan of stone circle
1 in: 10 ft
Pencil
558 mm x 380 mm

Sunkenkirk, Swinside
Stone Circle
SD18NE 5
SD17178818
DC4510
L1/3
Insc. Swinside, Sunkenkirk
Plan of stone circle
1/8 in: 1 ft
Black ink and pencil
560 mm x 382 mm

Whitemoss NE
Stone Circle
NY10SE 1
NY172 024
DC4518
L1/5
Insc. Burnmoor Circle D, 1959 Survey
Plan of stone circle
1/10 in: 1 ft
Blue ink and pencil
558 mm x 380 mm
1959

Whitemoss NE
(see above)
DC4519
L1/5
Insc. Burnmoor Circle D

Plan of stone circle
1/10 in: 1 ft
Blue ink and pencil
559 mm x 381 mm
1952

Whitemoss NE
(see above)
DC4515
L1/5
Insc. Burnmoor Circles
Plan showing the position of the stone circle in relation to the others with a chart showing circle centres as measured in 1966
3/4 in: 100 ft
Pencil
557 mm x 317 mm

Whitemoss NE
(see above)
DC4520
L1/5
Insc. Burnmoor, 1st Survey
Annotated plan showing the position of stone circle in relation to circles D and E.
1 in: 100 ft
Pencil
559 mm x 326 mm

Whitemoss SW
(see above)
DC4516
L1/5
Insc. Burnmoor Circle C, 1959 Survey plan of stone circle with chart showing adjusted distances between Theodosia stations
1/10 in: 1 ft
Blue ink and pencil
557 mm x 379 mm
1959

Whitemoss SW
(see above)
DC4517
L1/5
Insc. Burnmoor, Circle C
Plan of stone circle
1/10 in: 1 ft
Blue ink and pencil
559 mm x 382 mm
1952

Whitemoss SW
(see above)
DC4520
L1/5
Insc. Burnmoor, 1st Survey
Annotated plan showing position of stone circle in relation to circles C and E
1 in: 100 ft
Pencil
559 mm x 326 mm

Whitemoss SW
(see above)
DC4515
L1/5
Insc. Burnmoor Circles
Plan showing the position of the stone circle in relation to the others with chart showing circle centres as measured in 1966
3/4 in: 100 ft
Pencil
557 mm x 317 mm

LANCASHIRE

Druid's Temple
Stone Circle
SD27SE 23
SD292 739
DC4540
L5/1
Insc. Birkrigg Common
Plan of stone circle
1/8 in: 1 ft
Black ink and pencil
558 x 382 mm

WESTMORLAND

Castlehowe Scar
Stone Circle
NY51NE 6
NY587 154
DC4533
L2/11
Insc. Castlehowe Scar
Plan of stone circle
1/4 in: 1 ft
Black ink and pencil
561 mm x 377 mm

Cockpit (The)
Stone Circle
NY42SE 11
NY482 222
DC4532
L2/2
Insc. Tarnmoor, Ullswater
Plan of stone circle
1/8 in: 1 ft
Blue ink and pencil
560 mm x 382 mm

Gamelands
Stone Circle
NY60NW 8
NY640 081
DC4537
L2/14
Insc. Orton
Plan of stone circle
1 in: 20 ft
Black ink and pencil
562 mm x 384 mm

Gamelands
(see above)
DC4784
L2/14
Insc. Composite Survey of Four Circles.
Each reduced to the same diameter and orientated on major axis.
Plan
No scale
Black ink
363 mm x 284 mm
Tracing paper

Gunnerkeld
Stone Circle
NY51NE 4
NY568 177
DC4775
L2/10
Insc. Gunnerwell
Plan of stone circle.
Annotated 'Note by AST. I re-surveyed this and the farm is called Gunnerswell, pronounced Goonerwell. How did Aubrey Burl get…Keld?'
1/8 in: 1 ft
Black ink and pencil
559 mm x 384 mm

High Street
Stone Circle
NY41NE 2
NY45711925

DC4541
L2/3
Insc. High Street
Plan of stone circle
1/8 in: 1 ft
Pencil
558 mm x 380 mm

High Street
(see above)
DC4896
L2/3
Insc. High Street
Plan of stone circle
5/8 in: 5 ft
Black ink
308 mm x 271 mm
Plastic film

Iron Hill
Stone Circle
NY51SE 7
NY596 147
DC4534
L2/12
Insc. Harberwain
Plan of stone circle
1/8 in: 1 ft
Blue ink and pencil
560 mm x 381 mm

Iron Hill
(see above)
DC4535
L2/12
Insc. Harberwain
Plan of stone circle
1/8 in: 1 ft
Pencil
560 mm x 336 mm

Oddendale
Stone Circle
NY51SE 8
NY59211291
DC4536
L2/13
Insc. Oddendale
Anootated plan of stone circle
1/8 in: 1 ft
Black ink and pencil
561 mm x 382 mm

Appendix IV

MUSEUMS

THE FOLLOWING is a list of museums which have archaeological collections of the Neolithic and Bronze Ages, which will further an understanding of the period. Some of these are either directly associated with the stone circles or with the time in which they were constructed. Such collections serve to deepen and develop our experience of the time. They are the touchstones to a people who had direct knowledge of the monuments. Some of the collections are not on permanent display because much of the material from archaeological excavations would not be suitable. Indeed, many of the artefacts are exhibited occasionally in temporary exhibitions. But the museums do welcome public interest in any aspect of the collections, whether displayed or otherwise.

Most museums have a Collections or Exhibitions Officer who may be able to supply more detailed information concerning specific artefacts from the collections which relate to the time of the stone circles. Opening times and admission charges are subject to variation so do check on these before your visit to save disappointment. For further details visit:

www.lakesandcumbria.info/cumbrian/museums1.html

The Armitt Gallery, Museum and Library,
Rydal Road,
Ambleside,
Cumbria,
LA22 9BL.
Tel. 01539 431212
www.armitt.com

The Dock Museum,
North Road,
Barrow-in-Furness,
Cumbria,
LA14 2PW.
Tel, 01229 894444
www.dockmuseum.org.uk

Museum of Archaeology and Natural History.
Station Road,
Kendal,
Cumbria,
LA9 6BT.
Tel; 01539 721374
www.kendalmuseum.org.uk

Keswick Museum and Art Gallery,
Station Road,
Keswick,
Cumbria,
CA12 4NF.
Tel; 01768 773263
http.www.allerdale.gov.uk

Lancaster City Museum,
Market Square,
Lancaster,
LA1 1HT.
Tel. 01524 64637
h.moore.lcm@ednet.lancs.ac.uk

Penrith Museum,
Robinson's School,
Middlegate,
Penrith,
Cumbria,
CA11 7PT.
Tel. 01768 212228
www.eden.gov.uk

Ruskin Museum, Coniston,
The Institute,
Yewdale Road,
Coniston,
Cumbria.
Tel. 01539 41164
www.ruskinmuseum.com

Tullie House Museum and Art Gallery,
Castle Street,
Carlisle,
Cumbria,
CA3 8TP.
Tel. 01228 534781
www.tulliehouse.co.uk

The Beacon Whitehaven Museum,
West Strand,
Whitehaven,
Cumbria,
CA28 2LY.
Tel. 01946 592302
www.copelandbc.gov.uk

Appendix V

ADDENDUM

NOTE 1: The prehistoric environment was a significant factor in the locality of settlement. Water levels were much higher and estuaries more extensive. The valleys were inhospitable and poorly drained with large areas of wetlands, bogs and mud flats. The forest too was a wilderness which often proved hostile. The lowlands were a tangle of scrub and thicket with woodlands reaching to heights approximating with the line of bracken evident today. Only the higher fells and mountains remained clear of undergrowth. In many places the lowlands must have been difficult to access and the woodlands were a further visual restriction. The stone axe from the mountain hinterland was the tool first employed in the labour of clearing these badlands and making them more hospitable for settlement and cultivation. Within these clearances, usually on the higher and better drained lands, both settlement and the more enduring 'ritual' monuments were located according to their own strategies. Many of these clearances would later in time become tracts of unfertile moorland. The result of climate change and wetter conditions during the Bronze Age, when periods of heavy rain would wash away the minerals and nutrients from the over-cultivated soils.

NOTE 2: The larger stones are generally to be found on the inside of the monument. In 1985 aerial photography revealed a number of linear and curvilinear features on the moor and these were subsequently investigated resulting in a remarkable 44 new sites being identified - including an enclosure, a possible settlement site, banks, dykes, hollow ways, tracks and mounds. Amongst the most intriguing are some previously undocumented linear banks and dykes in the vicinity of the Kopstone which seem to have been laid out with regard to this monument; a series of hollow ways which coinciding with the Roman road of High Street suggesting that the Cockpit stone circle was located at 'a natural focal point in the landscape'; a number of mounds, possible burial mounds, one of these being located on the prominent summit of Heughscar hill. A division of the 'ritual' sites of the moor based upon an eyesight visibility of 1.5m above ground level with 'viewsheds' from the Cockpit and Site 5 was also considered. This seemed to suggest a spatial arrangement of the sites, the former being those in the ring cairn tradition with views to the N and W and the latter those with 'standing stones' facing S and E. It seemed significant that White Raise the largest and most prominent cairn in the locality occupied a pivotal position to both 'viewsheds'.